War & Peas

—ɯ—

Emotionally Aware Feeding - end the battle with picky eaters

Jo Cormack

First Printing, 2014
ISBN-13: 9780992771010
ISBN-10: 0992771013
Galanthus Press
Newark
UK

Contact: galanthuspress@gmail.com
Blog: www.ea-feeding.com
Cover design: www.joffandollie.co.uk

About the Author

Jo Cormack is a therapist specialising in working with children and young people. Born in London, England in 1977, she now lives in rural north Nottinghamshire with her husband and three daughters.

After a spell as a musician in a band, Jo became a youth worker in a residential hostel for homeless young people in Nottingham. She soon realised that the aspect of the work that she really loved involved listening to the young people talking about their experiences and their dreams. She decided to take this interest further and trained as a counsellor, getting a distinction in her MA at the University of Nottingham in 2007. In 2008, Jo won the BACP student research prize for her dissertation about counselling young homeless people, which led to the publication of her research in a peer reviewed journal. She is interested in writing about parenting from a psychological perspective, making research accessible to parents and carers.

In 2010, Jo and her husband, Adam, became registered foster carers. This was both a rewarding and a challenging experience, coming to an end when the couple's third child arrived and took up the last remaining corner of space in their small cottage. Jo is currently a full-time mother, writing whenever the opportunity presents itself.

Contents

Acknowledgements

Researching, developing and writing this book over the last five years has involved much coffee drinking and abandoned house-work on my part, but would not have been possible without the help of some significant people. I would like to thank Jane Woodnutt, Elise Clarke and Annabel Skelton for their brilliant proof-reading and editing input. Thanks to Jonathan Casciani (www.joffandollie.com) not only for the great cover design but also for the role he played in shaping my thinking about the project. Thanks to Tom Woodnutt for his un-flagging support and clarity of mind (www.feelingmutual.com) and to all the professionals who generously contributed to the book: Sue Wilson, Tasha Davis, Kathryn Barker, Jackie Vallance and Polly Walker. Thanks to Annabel Price for her useful input. A big thank you goes to the families who kindly allowed me to share their experiences and stories and I would also like to thank Margaret Dunkelman for her generous support. Finally, thanks to my husband Adam for his love, patience and eagle-eyed proof-reading skills.

I

Introduction

EAF stands for 'Emotionally Aware Feeding'. It is a new approach to feeding problems in young children. It involves teaching parents about the psychology of picky eating and showing them how to use that knowledge to improve their child's relationship with food. EAF helps parents to see that picky eating in small children is normal - it's how you choose to respond to it that makes all the difference.

If you think you think you may need help with your young child's picky eating, read on. Or perhaps you are a new parent or have a baby on the way. This book can help you to ensure that your child grows up with a positive relationship with food from the very beginning.

EAF can be reduced to a few straightforward rules and principles, explained throughout the book and summarised at the very end. The principles embody the theory behind EAF and the rules will help you use EAF on a day to day basis. EAF is simple but powerful. By changing the way you think about mealtimes, you can make dramatic changes to your child's eating behaviour.

The term 'picky eater' refers to a child who will only eat a limited range of foods and has an aversion to new foods, sometimes refusing meals altogether. Recent research shows that UK toddlers are the most likely in Europe to be picky eaters, with more than two thirds often refusing food and one in seven rejecting foods at every meal[1].In the USA, studies have found that between 20% and 50% of children were described by their parents as 'picky'[2]. The scale of this issue is enormous, affecting millions of families in richer countries worldwide.

Caring for a picky eater takes a huge emotional toll on parents and carers day in, day out. Worrying that your child is not eating enough and encountering a fight at every meal can be extremely upsetting. If you are finding mealtimes with your little one hard work and you want things to change, then this is the book for you. You are not alone and you *can* turn things around. It won't be easy but it will certainly be worth it. With EAF you can make mealtimes happy again.

Although at the moment, your day to day battles will probably be your central concern, it is important to think about the future too. If a child takes her problematic eating habits into adulthood, it can be socially crippling and can contribute to poor health. Cognitive therapist Daniel Mattila talks about some of the problems that adults who are picky eaters have to contend with[3], including difficulties in social and professional situations involving food. He also points out that food is one of life's chief pleasures. To miss out on experiencing new foods when travelling abroad, or when sharing meals prepared by friends and loved ones, is a serious loss.

Although scientists are still working on the precise time period when children's food habits are formed, it is generally agreed that it is in the first few years of life[4]. This is not to say that you cannot improve things when your child is older, but when a child is a toddler or pre-schooler, there is a window of opportunity when you still have a significant amount of influence over how she learns to respond to food.

EAF is not so much an instant solution as a new way of being, in relation to eating. Perhaps you are simply hoping to learn more about how to help your child develop good eating habits, or maybe you are at your wits' end, desperate for a way to make things better. Either way, EAF can make a difference to you.

How it all began

I am a therapist, former foster carer and mother of three and I am passionate about helping young children develop a healthy relationship with food. My interest in this area was first sparked when my eldest daughter was a toddler. I was a trainee counsellor working with young people with eating disorders.

I started to notice that there were similarities in the way that my young clients used food and the way that my two year old daughter was starting to test boundaries at the table.

As I got deeper into the issues these young people were grappling with, it became clear that, in their own individual ways, my clients were attempting to exert control over their environments by limiting what they ate. In every case, they felt out of control in other ways, perhaps because their parents were splitting up or they had experienced a stressful change such as a move to a new town. In other words, these teenagers felt powerless and found that controlling their diet gave them back a sense of power. This was a coping mechanism at a difficult time.

But it wasn't dysfunction that lay at the heart of my daughter's sense of powerlessness, it was her gradual realisation that there were things she wanted to do but couldn't - that there were boundaries. Working with the notions of power and control, I arrived at a theory which moves away from the conventional 'behavioural' approach to parenting in which 'good eating' is praised and 'bad eating' is treated as naughtiness. I realised that, in order to change negative eating behaviours, the focus had to be on the *feelings* that underpin them and EAF was born.

It is developmentally normal for children (at about the age of 24 months) to start saying "No!" in order to exert a little control in a world where they are beginning to realise that they are not in charge. They are experimenting with their own power as they develop a sense of self. I realised that this is what my daughter was demonstrating at the table. I began looking for ways to take the fight out of mealtimes so that she could no longer use her eating as a means of striving for autonomy. After several years of research into the academic literature on the subject, I developed the EAF model.

About *War and Peas*

If you are looking for a guide to nutrition then this is not the book for you. This is a book about *how* to feed your children, not *what*. I am assuming that you know how to offer a balanced meal and that if you want to know more about diet, you will know how to go about finding appropriate resources. This book is based on research, psychological theory and therapeutic principles. It will allow you to understand the mechanics of picky eating. Once you know *why* problem behaviours are happening, they are much easier to deal with. I aim to present research on this topic in an accessible way and provide easy to follow advice so that you can take practical steps towards solving your child's eating problems.

As a mother, I always want to understand what's behind my children's behaviour. Sometimes parenting books can be 'dumbed down' as though parents don't want the theory, just the tips. Equally I understand that not everyone is that way inclined, so except where a conceptual understanding of the subject matter is essential, the more theoretical sections of this book are presented in italics so that you can skip them if you prefer.

Throughout the text, I refer to children alternately as 'she' and 'he'. I also sometimes refer to 'mothers', especially in the context of feeding babies. This is because it is primarily the mother who concerns herself with this task. However, it is important to note that the ideas in this book are relevant to you whatever your gender and family set-up.

The Contributors

Various professionals have contributed to this book, sharing their experience and advice. Again, these sections are in italics so that you can skip them if you prefer. They include Tasha Davis, a family and relationship therapist and specialist family support worker, Sue Wilson.

Throughout the book there are examples of some of the things parents have shared with me about their experiences. All of these are genuine and included with permission, although names have been changed if requested. There is also a more detailed case-study which illustrates how EAF has helped one family who have generously allowed me to write about my work with them.

You will come across several short lists of questions entitled 'Time for reflection' as you read 'War and Peas'. These are designed to guide you through the aspects of EAF that involve examining your own habits, feelings and experiences in relation to food and feeding.

Health warning

First and foremost, it is important to stress that if you have any serious worries about your child's eating, there are professionals available to you who can be a vital source of help and support. If you are at all anxious about your child's weight or growth, it is essential that you take these concerns to your health care provider. This book is absolutely not intended as an alternative to medical intervention when that is required. It is also important to understand that EAF is an approach designed for healthy children. It is not appropriate if your child has been diagnosed with a particular psychological or physical problem that affects her growth or weight gain.

For my non-UK readers, I apologise for the references to the UK health care and education systems. For my American readers, when I talk about GPs and health visitors, this would translate as 'pediatrician'. Whatever the system where you live, the message is the same - if you have any concerns about your child, go and see your health care provider.

EAF is not a quick fix. You have to be really committed to doing things differently and this will not be easy. If your child has firmly entrenched negative habits in relation to food, things will probably get worse before they get better. Your child will probably test you by pushing even harder at any new boundaries you impose, in order to establish whether they are negotiable or not. It helps to expect this, so that you can find the strength to persevere.

SED and food refusal

Occasionally, a child's relationship with food is so problematic that it goes beyond what would be described as plain 'picky eating'. SED (selective eating disorder) is a label used by some medical professionals to describe cases where children exhibit extreme pickiness that is felt to go beyond the realms of 'normal'. Psychiatric conditions are classified in a manual used by doctors and psychiatrists called the DSM V. SED is not included in the DSM V or its predecessor, the DSM IV. However, the Royal College of Psychiatrists suggest that it is a descriptor that clinicians find useful, although there are no official diagnostic criteria. A child who suffers from SED will eat only a very narrow range of foods and will usually be healthy and of normal weight.

Food refusal is also not in the DSM V. Clinicians use it to describe a child who avoids food in an inconsistent way, perhaps in the presence of a particular person or at particular times[56]. If a medical professional has suggested that your child is suffering from food refusal or SED and their weight and growth is normal, EAF may be helpful but **only use it with your doctor's approval**. There are also several other labels that doctors use to describe children's eating problems but they are outside the remit of this book.

How to use this book

It is important that you *don't do anything differently* until you have read the entire book. You need to have a thorough understanding of how EAF works as a whole system in order to put it into place successfully. You may find that some of the rules and principles resonate with you more than others. This is fine, but in order for significant change to occur, you need to follow all of them consistently, otherwise you may be giving mixed messages to your child.

At the heart of EAF is the idea that your own attitudes to food play a role in the formation of your child's attitudes. Before you read any further, think about whether you are ready to explore these. For some people this can be really challenging and even frightening. If this is true for you, it would be a good idea to talk to someone you trust about these issues, or even seek therapy if you feel you need to.

At the end of each chapter there is a summary of the key ideas presented. At the end of the book there is a crib-sheet summarising the principles and rules central to EAF so that you can refer to it at a glance when necessary.

Are you ready?

If you still feel that you are ready for a challenge and want to put an end to picky eating and tears at the table, read on.

II

What is normal?

If you have concerns about your child's picky eating, you may feel very much alone. It may feel as though other families don't have the same challenges and can't understand what life is like for you. Whether this is true for you, or whether you know lots of other parents who are worried about the subject, it's important that you understand that **picky eating is normal**. It is normal from a developmental point of view - in other words, it is a natural stage that many children go through as they grow up. It can also be seen as normal from an evolutionary perspective - an aspect of how the human race has learnt to adapt to its environment over millennia.

The evolutionary perspective

The theory goes that toddlers are innately programmed to avoid food-stuffs that are unfamiliar. Let's go back to prehistory, when people lived a simpler existence and the drive to survive over-rode everything else. Back in our hunter-gathering days, once a child became mobile, his safety would have been seriously compromised had he put every leaf and berry that he came across into his mouth. Before too long, he would surely have eaten something poisonous and that would have been that.

We have now adapted to the point where our children cannot easily access toxic substances and so this fear of the unfamiliar no longer serves a purpose. However, a distrust of alien food remains[7]. It makes sense that this kicks in after the age of about 12 months, when babies discover the possibilities that come with their new-found mobility.

From an evolutionary point of view, children who avoided eating anything that they did not think of as a tried and tested food-stuff stood a better chance of survival. This fits in with the very visually driven rejection of foods demonstrated by some toddlers. Colour and textural appearance often seem to be important. For example, a child may only accept brown food or dry food, as though different colours and textures were threatening.

Just as the beginning of unfamiliar food avoidance coincides with early mobility, so this phase normally passes as children become old enough to learn about what is safe and what isn't, at around three to five years of age. I know one five year old living in the countryside, who is fascinated by which hedgerow plants are edible and which are not. Her brain is clearly very able to make and enjoy these distinctions. Perhaps, just like her hunter-gatherer ancestors, this little forager is practising a skill that is inherent to the survival of the human race.

The developmental perspective

The second reason why picky eating is normal is that it is part of a developmental process. In other words, scientists can track children's relationship with food in line with their normal developmental trajectory[8]. A baby has a simple need for food. She needs only one source of nourishment -milk - and her desire for milk is driven by hunger and the need for comfort. Later, her nutritional needs become more complex and she begins eating solids. Throughout the weaning process, she is gradually introduced to new tastes and textures. At about 18 months, she will probably be able to eat much the same food as the rest of the family. It is around this age that 'food neophobia' (a fear of new foods) may emerge as she enters a phase where she is grappling with issues of independence and autonomy[9]. At this stage, picky eating is absolutely normal.

Researchers studying picky eating in toddlers found that "During the 24 to 36 month period, autonomy and independence issues about foods likely contributed to the picky eater phenomenon. Any new food experience can become a power struggle between parent and child."[10]

The fight for autonomy or 'the terrible-twos'

I have always felt that the 'terrible-twos' are more like the 'terrible-one-and-a-halfs', as that is the age I have observed the tantrums and boundary battles beginning in my family. Whenever it starts, it is a testing phase for even the most patient of parents.

This time in a child's life is characterised by mood swings, a desire for independence and moments of extreme frustration, coupled of course with the delightful emergence of an individual personality. Toddlers oscillate between needing to be babied and wanting to do it all themselves and their skills do not always match their ambitions. They have things to say but cannot find the words. They have a plan but lack the cognitive ability to appreciate that it's never going to work. They are such busy, active little people that they wear themselves out and don't have the emotional resilience to cope with the ensuing tiredness.

A two year old's favourite word is "NO!" He is beginning to perceive that the adults around him have control and he's experimenting with this. Throughout this book, I refer to the 'power play' that small children engage in. Used in relation to an adult, this term would have negative connotations implying that a person was manipulative or malign. Used in relation to a child, however, seeking power is a normal part of learning about where the boundaries are. This is a healthy process, giving him a sense that his world is safe and contained. However, it can be a painful stage to experience as his desire for autonomy is so strong that it can result in extreme emotional outbursts.

Getting stuck

Given all of the challenging aspects of this developmental stage, it is no wonder that some of them manifest themselves during meals. It is absolutely normal for a toddler to express extreme defiance at the table, rejecting food or having a tantrum because some aspect of it is not 'right'. My eldest daughter used to get extremely upset as a two year old if her food was ever broken - a cracker in two pieces would drive her to distraction!

A toddler will frequently choose the dinner table as one of his battle grounds for autonomy. Perhaps he wants to do everything himself, pushing at the boundaries and refusing to eat in a bid to establish independence. Perhaps he is trying to gain control, or express his likes and dislikes as a demonstration of his own emergent identity.

One of the most important things to remember at this tricky time is to remain in control of your own emotions. If you get very anxious or angry, your child can get stuck in this phase because she is getting so many pay-offs from her oppositional behaviour. We will look at this in some detail in the next chapter. If you can weather this temporary storm, it will pass. Stay focused but relaxed and don't worry.

Easier said than done?

Any reasonable parent who feels that their child has a problem with food and so may not be getting all the nutrients that he needs *will* be feeling anxious. Staying relaxed and not worrying, then, is a tall order. First, check that the problem is one that you can manage yourself without expert professional input. Go to your health visitor and have your child weighed and measured. The chances are his height and weight will be normal. Research shows that the majority of children whose parents consider that they have an eating problem will suffer no adverse consequences in terms of growth[11].

Secondly, respect your child's decisions about what she needs to eat. Let her take responsibility for getting enough goodness from her diet. This is called 'self-regulation'. Your job is to offer healthy, balanced meals at regular times. Her job is to recognise her body's cues and eat what she actually needs. This may be different from what you think she needs. This is an idea that we will explore in more detail in Chapter 9.

At the age of one, a child's growth rate declines suddenly. This is coupled with a corresponding decrease in appetite. From one onwards, her appetite will fluctuate, sometimes dramatically. At times, she needs to eat a lot to support a growth spurt, or because she is burning calories as she tries out new skills. At other times, she is hardly hungry and seems to get by on next to nothing. Whatever stage of growth she is at, a child of normal weight will self-regulate, her body ensuring that it gets exactly the right amount of energy for that particular stage[12].

Protecting children from hunger

EAF has several separate but overlapping strands, all of which will be expanded upon and explained in detail as the book progresses. First, emotions need to be separated from eating. Children's eating behaviour needs to be driven by physical signals (i.e. appetite) not by external pressure from parents. Part of this separation involves children understanding that if they choose not to eat, this will be respected. However, if they feel hungry later, they'll have to live with that.

We need to trust our children to listen to their bodies. For this to happen, they have to be allowed to experience hunger. I don't mean the kind of hunger that comes of deprivation and self-denial, but the natural hunger that is part of the day's rhythm. Before a meal, we feel hungry and ready to eat. After a meal, we feel full.

There are several reasons why a parent may want to protect their child from hunger. Perhaps they experienced true hunger as a child and don't ever want their child to have to feel anything like they did. Perhaps they find their child's behaviour when he is hungry hard to manage. Perhaps they feel that it is part of their role to ensure that their child does not experience discomfort. It is socially very normal to offer children snacks but the message that comes with this is that if a child is starting to feel hungry he needs immediate relief. Not only is it okay for your child to feel hungry before a meal, it is essential to the process of self-regulation. If you practice EAF, you will sometimes have a hungry child.

Perhaps this seems a little draconian, with resonances of Victorian children being 'sent to bed without supper'. However, EAF is not punitive. There is no place for blame or anger here, just a calm explanation that leaving food is a choice your child has made of which hunger is the consequence. As long as you are consistently offering appropriate meals, letting your child choose not to eat them is okay. However, it is important to clarify that hunger caused by *not* offering your children appropriate meals is not okay and is tantamount to neglect.

Summary

- Picky eating is a normal phase, from both an evolutionary and a developmental perspective

- Children are grappling with issues of autonomy and control during the toddler years - don't let these battles play out at the table

- If you can stay laid back and weather this phase, it will pass. If you respond to it with lots of emotion and attention, a child may get 'stuck' there

- We try to protect children from hunger for many reasons - in fact, feeling hungry before a meal is a good thing

III

Attention, please!

Anyone who has experienced the stress and anxiety that come of worrying about a child's eating will be familiar with the wide range of approaches parents may use to try to improve things.

Cajoling

Cajoling involves gentle persuasion, often with a sense of playfulness and fun, for example, "here comes the aeroplane". Cajoling can refer to the food itself: "try it, it's delicious".

Reasoning

Some parents focus on their child's nutritional needs: "eat it because you need your vitamins" or "eating your vegetables will make you big and strong".

Incentivising

Children are often offered rewards for eating: "try your cabbage and you can have a sticker on your chart".

Comparison

This is when other people's eating is used as a means of persuasion: "look at your big brother eating it all up".

The authoritarian approach

Sometimes a parent gives in to feelings of anger and demands that the child eats, perhaps coupled with threats of sanctions: "eat it because I say so!"

Negotiation

This involves bargaining with your child: "eat three mouthfuls then you can get down", "ten more peas then you can have pudding".

Pleading

Often this can be associated with parental anxiety. If you are extremely worried about your child's eating, you may find yourself pleading with her: "please just try one little bite…for me?"

Every parent who has ever wanted their child to eat better will recognise at least one of the above strategies. Each and every example involves giving her **attention** for eating pickily or refusing food. With EAF you will learn how to stop doing this. First, we'll consider why this is so vital. We will look at both negative and positive attention, what these mean for your child and how to break the relationship between eating and attention that is likely to be entrenched in families with a picky eater.

Research supports the idea that encouraging children to eat can paradoxically result in making the problem even worse. A study of just under 1000 British children in their first 13 months showed that when mothers put pressure on their children to eat, rather than encouraging them to be less picky, it actually made their eating worse and even resulted in the subsequent avoidance of food[13]. Similarly, another study found that "…if mothers use rewards, prodding or punishment to encourage eating, this may contribute to the picky eater phenomenon"[14]

What is negative attention?

To understand negative attention, let's look briefly at what positive attention entails. Positive attention means paying attention to your child because he is behaving well. For example, he's colouring quietly at the table and co-operating with his younger brother, so you spend a few minutes asking him about his picture, praising his behaviour and artistic efforts. This is what is known as 'catching your child being good', a phrase used by Dr Sal Severe in his book 'How to behave so your children will too!'[15]

We'd all like to have time to do this more often. It's just too easy to take advantage of the moments when the children are quietly amusing themselves to go and cook the dinner, make an important phone call or worm the cat. However, every time you succeed at catching your child being good, you reinforce that behaviour by rewarding him with a few minutes of your attention.

Negative attention is the opposite of this. It is the kind of attention every parent is familiar with: focusing on your child because he is *not* behaving well. Picture the scene, Max is helping his little sister do a jigsaw. Mum notices that the children are amusing themselves nicely so gets on with something in another room. Then she hears screams and Max is pulling his little sister's hair. In comes Mum to sort the situation out and suddenly, Max has her attention.

The important thing to remember is that **children prefer negative attention to no attention**. This is counter-intuitive for adults - who would rationally choose to be attacked rather than to be ignored? For children, however, it's part of their in-built survival strategy. They quickly learn how to get negative attention with their behaviour and very soon, you're stuck in a vicious circle whereby they behave badly, you give negative attention and so they do it again.

The situation is self-perpetuating. You become increasingly less likely to give positive attention because the atmosphere has become combative and everyone's fed-up. This is one way a negative pattern of relating can build up. If you start to notice that every exchange with your child is cross and critical, perhaps you have got stuck in this negative place.

Sometimes, children will misbehave because they feel it's expected of them. To put this back in the context of mealtimes, if a child is used to being criticised at the table and the parent is used to him misbehaving, both slip into these roles as soon as the meal starts. It's like he thinks "right, now we're at the table, this is how I get attention from Mum" and the complaints about food begin.

It is very hard as a parent to change this dynamic because pleasant conversation doesn't come easily when you're feeling annoyed and frustrated. Also, once the child has started the bad behaviour, it's much easier for him to continue than to snap out of it. Part of EAF is a focus on the social aspects of eating where positive interactions and a relaxed atmosphere at mealtimes become the norm.

Why EAF is different

EAF is very different from many conventional parenting approaches in that eating is not seen as a behaviour to be altered. Eating is one of life's everyday functions and is not in the same category as desirable behaviours such as sharing well, being polite, tidying toys away etc. With EAF, the focus is taken *away* from eating rather than it being highlighted with praise or criticism.

Specialist family support worker, Sue Wilson, talks about the notion of 'overpraise' when she works with parents. Sue says that by praising a child for doing everyday activities like eating, sleeping and toileting, they become potential sources of power for the child, in other words she can make decisions about how she does them in order to elicit an emotional response from her parent.

Sue believes that we should expect children to manage these activities without fuss, in an age-and-stage appropriate way. By saving praise for situations where a child has made an effort to change a specific behaviour, like tidying up toys or sharing well, your words will have more meaning. Used sparingly but genuinely, praise can have a real impact. In other words, when it comes to praising your children, less is more.

Conventional parenting techniques that I refer to as 'behavioural parenting', involve deciding what behaviours are desired and rewarding them, coupled with deciding what behaviours are not desired and using sanctions to put a stop to them. For example, TV's 'Supernanny' who recommends clear sanctions and reward systems to solve unwanted behaviour, advises on her website:

"Make 'taking a bite of everything on my plate' or 'sitting at the table until I'm finished' categories in your child's reward scheme and remember positive attention and praise are the best rewards." (The Supernanny Team)[16]

Let's think about what message this is giving to the child. It is telling her that eating her food is a behaviour that you require from her. This gives her the power to choose not to carry out that behaviour (i.e. to be fussy or refuse food) in order to get an emotional response from you.

With EAF, manners are separated from eating. Supernanny's recommendation to treat 'sitting at the table nicely' as a desired behaviour, perhaps to be recognised with a reward chart, could be a useful one. However, if eating is treated in the same way, it encourages children to use food as a means to personal power. We will take a closer look at manners later in the book.

There is nothing fundamentally wrong with behavioural parenting as a technique, but to think about eating as a behaviour to be modified is mistaken. Instead, parents can help their child to see food as something to be enjoyed and to feel grateful for, thus ending its role as an emotional currency. If you can encourage your child to make choices about what she eats based on the consequences for her, as opposed to gaining emotional leverage over you, you have almost won the battle.

These consequences relate to the physical sensations of fullness and hunger. With EAF, natural appetite is the thing that motivates a child to eat, not the parent. Understanding the role of appetite is a fundamental part of this approach and will be explored in detail later.

Back in the day…

Looking back to post-war Britain in the 1950s, anecdotal evidence suggests that picky eating wasn't really an issue in those days. Yes, rules at the table were stricter, but on the whole, children ate what they were given, were always hungry at mealtimes and were grateful for the food on their plates. In the 50s, it would have been unthinkable to describe a child enthusiastically eating his dinner as an example of 'good behaviour'.

When resources were scarce, people were just glad of what they had. One 'baby-boomer' I spoke to remembers that when she was at school in the 50s, a child leaving something on his plate during school dinners was a rarity that would be reacted to with amazement by the other children.

Nowadays, although we are in challenging economic times, most children have enough food to eat. They have the luxury of being able to refuse food, knowing that they'll be given alternatives or will be able to fill up on snacks later. Eating has become something adults want children to do, not something everyone does simply to survive.

If appetite is the motivating factor and a child eats because she is hungry, emotion does not enter into it. If pleasing a parent (or getting the negative attention discussed earlier) is the motivating factor, behaviour around food becomes complicated as it turns into a very effective emotional lever.

The first step towards changing this dynamic is contained in the first principle of EAF:

EAF principle 1

- Avoid either praising or criticising how or what your child is eating

Praising your child for eating tells him that it is a behaviour that you want from him. If you avoid praise, you will weaken this notion. If he doesn't believe that eating particular foods is something you want him to do, he can't make a decision about whether to comply or not in order to get a particular response from you. In other words, if you praise him for eating well, this gives him a message that he can get attention from you by choosing not to eat. By avoiding criticism, you stop giving him negative attention for picky eating, so he no longer gets any pay-offs from choosing to behave like that.

With EAF, the choices your child makes about how much of his meal he eats elicit no emotional response from you whatsoever. He begins to take responsibility for his decisions as he experiences the consequences - rewards in the form of a parental reaction are no longer available. Once you've conveyed the message that it doesn't matter to you what your child eats, you've taken away the bulk of his incentives to refuse food. In short, you are working towards a situation where **your child's motivation to eat is internal and physiological, not external and emotional.**

It can feel very uncomfortable not to praise your child for eating well, especially if she has previously been a poor eater so any improvement in this area feels like a big achievement. One way round this is to give indirect positive attention. What this means is that, rather than direct positive attention like "Wow, Katie, you've eaten all your cabbage! That's fantastic!" you can quietly notice that Katie is eating her cabbage and say something along the lines of "You seem to be really enjoying that cabbage, Katie! I love it too…" followed by some more warm attention on a different topic: "so tell me about what you were watching on TV".

This way, you are acknowledging Katie's enjoyment of her food and it doesn't become the 'elephant in the room'. You are giving her positive attention in terms of a social exchange rather than praise that focuses on her eating. The better you get at creating a relaxed atmosphere at mealtimes and taking the spotlight off what your child is eating, the more she will automatically start to experiment with new foods. However, this will only happen once the pressure is off and dinner time power games are a thing of the past.

Summary

- Positive attention means 'catching your child being good'

- Negative attention means giving your child attention for misbehaving

- By no longer giving your child either positive or negative attention for how he eats, you can begin to break down the connection between food consumption and power that can lie beneath picky eating

- **EAF principle 1**
  Avoid either praising or criticising how or what your child is eating

IV

Food and you

How can something as natural as feeding your child be so very emotive? Why is it that so much anxiety, anger and even sadness can be generated at the table, together with a little happiness thrown in for when meals do go your way? When you're a parent, if the basics aren't right - eating, sleeping, toileting - daily life can feel like an uphill struggle.

Starting at the very beginning, wanting to feed and nurture your child is a primal instinct, a fundamental drive without which mankind would cease to exist. Right from the start, there's so much internal and external pressure to get it 'right'. Having got the minor hurdle of giving birth to your baby out of the way, the next challenge is to feed her.

From other people, there is the debate over breast versus bottle, with the potential to sow seeds of guilt in women who choose not to breast-feed, or are unable to. Then there's anxiety about whether your baby is feeding enough and the constant checking of growth charts and visits to the clinic. The pressure a mother puts herself under to feed her baby 'properly' is overwhelming. Any fears about getting this wrong can be very powerful.

A 2007 study examined how the choices a woman makes about feeding her baby can take on a moral aspect and even contribute to her sense of identity. Feelings reported by participants who ended up not breast-feeding, included a sense of failure (32%), guilt (33%) and anxiety about the baby's health (20%). One participant, Rebecca, said "You're such a failure because all you've got to do for this baby is feed it and if you just can't do that, or you're having problems with that, you must be rubbish"[17]

Women who have had problems feeding their babies early on may find that anxieties about 'getting it right' spill over into the next phase when the baby is ready for solids. However, even if you found it all plain sailing in the early days, weaning has its own challenges.

It can be an exciting milestone, but sometimes all that build-up and thought about what to introduce and when can lead to a bit of an anti-climax when lovingly prepared, organic sweet potato puree is forcibly rejected and ends up all over the walls. Even for parents with no issues around food and feeding, this can be frustrating and disappointing. However, if you factor in early challenges with your baby such as problems with breast-feeding or anxiety about her weight gain, it's easy to see how something that may superficially seem natural and straightforward can become a source of guilt and worry.

Your relationship with food

Your history with your baby can influence how you feel about her eating later on, but so can your own food-history before she was even a twinkle in your eye. Before you can really examine what's going on with your child's eating, you need to look at your own relationship with food. As a society, we tend to locate the problem in the child, labelling them 'fussy', 'picky', 'difficult' or 'naughty'. This can be easier than looking at how underlying ideas and feelings in the family may have contributed to the problem.

It is important to say, however, that it's certainly not helpful to go to the other extreme, dumping everything at the feet of the parent. In fact, it is fruitless trying to blame either the adult or the child for problematic eating. It is more constructive to just concentrate on putting things right. To try to establish who's 'fault' it is would be an over-simplification of a complex situation.

Thinking about families systemically

Family systems theory is based on the idea that, rather than addressing the problems of one member of a family individually, problems need to be tackled by looking at the 'system' that the individual is part of, i.e. his family. Each member of the system affects the others and problems and solutions are co-created.

Family and relationship therapist, Tasha Davis says "It's amazing how useful looking at the family as a whole can be, whether you're trying to deal with eating problems or any other behavioural issue. Spending time thinking about how each member of the family is affected by the problem and maybe even contributes to it can be very powerful."

I worked with a family where the three year old boy refused new foods and was extremely picky, always having a special meal prepared for him that was different from his siblings' meals. He had been diagnosed as hypersensitive and the problem had been located in him alone. Whilst this diagnosis was no doubt valid, using a systemic approach proved very useful. When we talked about the food habits of the rest of the family, it turned out that his father had coeliac disease, meaning he couldn't eat wheat products. He too had special meals prepared for him.

With this information in mind, it turned out to be very productive to understand part of the little boy's problems as an attempt to be like daddy and have special meals. Furthermore, the little boy appeared genuinely frightened of new foods that he did not consider 'safe'. This makes total sense in the context of living with a coeliac father who had to avoid certain types of food in case he had a severe physical reaction.

Time for reflection

The following exercise is designed to help you to think about your relationship with food. Once you have a good understanding of your own 'food legacy', you can begin to consider how it might be affecting your child and your reactions to your child's approach to food.

You can try these activities by yourself if you'd prefer, or, if you are tackling problematic eating as a couple, it can lead to some very productive conversations if you can look at them with your partner. Write down your answers individually then discuss them. This can be quite emotional, so make sure it's the right time and you have the time and space to process whatever comes up.

1) In your family when you were growing up, what beliefs around food and mealtimes can you remember?

2) In two separate lists, note down all your positive and negative feelings about food

3) What is your worst childhood memory about food?

4) What is your happiest childhood memory about food?

5) Describe how you would like your child's relationship with food to be.

6) Is this the same as how you would describe your relationship with food? If not, how does it differ?

For many people (like Susie in the case study included towards the end of the book) the link between how they were parented and how they parent is not immediately obvious. Sometimes we reproduce the bad bits along with the good, sometimes we are extremely conscious that we do not want our children to experience what we experienced in childhood. Either way, our histories shape us as parents.

For some, food really is the enemy. More than one million people in the UK[18] and many millions in the US[19] are affected by an eating disorder and many more have battled with food in one way or another. If you feel that you have any serious issues in this area, it's really worth getting some help. This is not just something you should do for yourself, but for your children too. It will enhance your ability to parent and help you ensure that your own challenges don't begin to affect your children. There are resources at the end of this book that can point you in the direction of further support.

How do you feel?

Having established that your beliefs and feelings about food can affect how you approach your child's eating, let's look at how these might manifest themselves. It's simple - if you are anxious about your child not eating enough, he will 'catch' that anxiety and start to experience it himself. Children are emotional sponges. They may not understand the feelings around them but they certainly feel them. Once you become anxious, your child will become anxious too and will probably dig his heels in further, thus making you more anxious and so the situation escalates as the emotions feed each other and intensify.

Exactly the same thing happens with anger. If you have a small child, you will no doubt have experienced the situation where your toddler expresses frustration and anger. If you respond with frustration and anger, this turns up your child's emotional thermostat until you are stoking one another's negative feelings and everyone has lost control. I know I've been there. Equally, you have probably experienced the power of staying calm and unemotional in the face of your toddler's rage. If you respond calmly to a tantrum it takes the wind out of your child's sails and the same applies at the table.

Sometimes your emotional reaction to your child can be quite subtle and you have to take a moment to step outside yourself and assess what's going on for you before you can work out which emotions you are experiencing. For example, you may be feeling more and more frustrated because each time you offer your child food, she screams 'NO!!' and spits it out. On the surface you might seem positive, trying "the train's going into the tunnel…", or smiling, but inwardly you're screaming. Your child is experiencing the inward scream far more intensely than the surface niceties. Her emotions intensify and the vicious circle continues. When practicing EAF, learning how to stay genuinely calm is essential.

EAF principle 2

- Stay calm and upbeat, keeping anger and anxiety away from the table

The only way to do this effectively is to learn to recognise your own feelings and take steps to relax. Perhaps you are feeling angry and need a moment to cool down. Perhaps you are feeling anxious and are beginning to catastrophise. This is where your initial worry about your child's eating gets blown up in your imagination to the worst-case scenario where he's losing weight and is malnourished, etc. Recognising emotions comes more easily to some people than to others. Some people find that they can recognise how they're feeling retrospectively, but not whilst they are in the grip of their emotions.

If you find it hard to stop and assess how you are feeling 'in the moment' you can try the following simple approach: once you have realised that you are not happy and relaxed, start to focus on what's going on inside your body. How is your breathing? Is it shallow? Does your heart feel like it's beating very fast? Are you tense? What about your voice, is it louder, tight-sounding perhaps? And your body language - are you in your child's personal space? Are you gesticulating? This kind of self-observation will help to loosen the grip of those feelings and enable you to identify them too. With practice, it will also help you spot them earlier, so you have more control over them before they escalate.

Watching your child's body language and listening to his tone of voice will also give you clues. Once you have identified his emotions, ask yourself, am I feeling that too? Luckily, a calm, upbeat mood is just as infectious as an angry, anxious one, so if you can manage to authentically create that at mealtimes, your child will soon start to absorb it and reflect it back. Remember, it has to be real. You can't fake it, because what's important is what your child is picking up subconsciously, not the surface words and smiles through gritted teeth.

Summary

- The urge to feed your child successfully is a basic human instinct and problems in this area can be deeply distressing

- Don't waste time blaming either yourself or your child for her eating habits. Family Systems theory teaches us to look at things from a 'whole family' perspective

- If you want to address your child's eating behaviours you need to look at your own relationship with food

- In order to help your child, you need to have a genuine awareness of your own emotional state during meals. Having an insight into your own feelings will give you some measure of control over them, enabling you to follow this next EAF principle

- **EAF principle 2**
  Stay calm and upbeat, keeping anger and anxiety away from the table

V

The EAF rules

Putting theory into practice

So now you understand the need to a) not focus on your child's eating with positive or negative attention and b) keep meal-times happy and relaxed, understanding and managing your own feelings. Let's consider how to achieve this in practical terms.

EAF is not about endless rules, but sticking to three key ones will help you make some crucial changes. Here are the first two:

1) **To avoid making food an issue before anyone's even sat down, never give any options - put everything on everyone's plate, in age appropriate portions**

2) **It is fine for your child to leave anything he or she doesn't want to eat, but there will be no alternatives and no unscheduled snacks later**

This way, you're giving him a choice about what he eats and leaving no room for dramas about it. There's no argument to be had because you're not fighting with him - he has a choice and will have to live with the consequences. Equally, if he chooses to eat only one mouthful of his meal, he can't fill up on snacks later.

It's important to respect the fact that children, like adults, do have genuine food aversions, but by giving them a bit of everything then letting them choose whether they eat it or not, you immediately take some of the drama out of the mealtime. Once children know that a hard and fast rule is in place, they won't bother to challenge it. For example, if you have a rule that sweets are only allowed on a Friday evening, once your child really understands that you are not prepared to be flexible on that, she won't bother to ask for them at other times.

Serving everyone everything is not to deny that children, just like adults, do genuinely dislike certain foods. In fact, not only are food aversions very real, scientists have discovered that they can be genetically determined. For example, the catchily named gene TAS2R38 is thought to be responsible for a dislike of Brussels sprouts. People with this gene experience a chemical called PTC (found in the cabbage family) as particularly bitter. People without it cannot taste PTC, hence the well-known split between sprout fanatics and sprout phobics.

You need to walk a delicate line between on the one hand, potentially disregarding elements of who your child is as a person by ignoring her likes and dislikes and on the other, making them into a major issue. If you talk about them all the time, the labels begins to stick - tell enough people enough times that Maya hates peas and sure enough, Maya will avoid peas assiduously. The best approach is not to dwell on what your child says she dislikes, just keep on offering it and stay relaxed when she chooses to leave it.

Another advantage of giving your child whatever's on the menu, regardless of how likely you think she is to eat it, is that, as we will see later, researchers have found that it can take many presentations of a certain food before a child will start to accept it. This means that you might get some pleasant surprises when one day she starts to spontaneously try new things and step out of her culinary comfort zone.

You may worry that when you serve a picky child the same meal as the rest of the family she will only eat a small part of it, or even leave the entire meal if her food dislikes are very extensive. Initially, she probably will. But once the focus has moved away from what's going into her mouth and everyone has started to relax a bit, the chances are she'll slowly start trying new things.

A key part of EAF is using your child's natural appetite, the idea being that if no alternative is offered, he'll feel hungry so he'll eat. This is something we'll look at more closely in Chapter 9. Equally, he might not feel hungry because he may not need as much food that day as you assume he does. Again, this is something we'll be returning to in more detail.

What does success look like?

If you give your child an unfamiliar or previously rejected food, you may feel that this has been a wasted effort if it remains uneaten at the end of the meal. Redefine your notions of success. Even smelling or putting a new food near the mouth is progress. If your child is simply tolerating it on the plate and becoming more familiar with its appearance, smell and texture, this is a baby-step towards acceptance. If she doesn't make a fuss, but simply leaves it on the side, this is a small victory - maybe next time she'll put it to her mouth or even take a bite. Never comment, never criticise and never praise her for any of this, just notice it and feel a step closer to your goal.

Attention again…

Finally, the idea that everyone gets a bit of everything, ties in with the objective of not giving children attention or power in response to picky behaviour. If your child is getting 'special' dinners with food arranged in a particular way or food that is different from everyone else's, he is potentially using this to exercise a little control which, as we saw in the last chapter, may be at the heart of the problem.

If you have clear, simple rules that everyone understands and that you NEVER deviate from, your child will soon realise that pleading to have his crusts cut off is pointless. He can choose to leave them, it won't be an issue, but it is certainly not an effective way to get attention. Thus you can move on to more constructive ways of giving your child attention at the table, which we will look at later.

Summary

Two of the three EAF rules:

1) To avoid making food an issue before anyone's even sat down, never give any options - put everything on everyone's plate, in age appropriate portions

2) It is fine for your child to leave anything they don't want to eat, but there will be no alternatives and no unscheduled snacks later

VI

Good food, bad food

In the last chapter we touched briefly on the many and varied ways parents try to encourage their children to eat. One of the most common approaches is to hold the pudding hostage: "eat up your greens or you won't get any pudding". Research shows that this tactic makes picky eating worse. If you make a child eat a particular food before she is allowed dessert, she will eat more of it at that particular meal, but her dislike of it will increase[20]. EAF is about establishing positive habits for life, not getting your child to eat healthy food in the short-term, despite the longer-term consequences.

Looking to the future, once no-one is there saying '*if* you eat X you can have Y', a person is likely to choose the foods they prefer to eat. If you have been brought up to be in habit of making your own, healthy choices about food, this will hopefully endure. However, if someone else has been making the choices for you, making sweet 'reward' foods dependent on eating 'hard work' foods like vegetables, once you plan your own menus, who wouldn't opt to miss out on vegetables simply because they could?

In another study, researchers took two snacks that they decided were equally appealing to children. They told the children participating that they could have one if they ate the other, thereby setting one type of snack up as the 'hard work' food and the other as the 'reward'. Sure enough, the children ended up preferring the 'reward' snack, demonstrating that adults can influence a child's food preferences based on how they talk about and present food[21].

Not only does the 'pudding rule' set up bad habits later in life, it is also an example of a problematic split that can be set up between 'good' food and 'bad' food. As soon as you introduce the notion that some foods are a chore and others are a reward, not only do you reinforce the idea that sweet, unhealthy foods are desirable and healthy foods are not, you also mix eating and feelings (of which, more later).

An article in the UK press[22] revealed that one in three parents deals with fussy eaters by bribing them with sweets. What message does this give a child? It gives her the emotional lever we looked at in Chapter 3. She gets a clear message that Mum is desperate for her to eat her peas - so desperate that she is offering her sweets to do so. This presents her with an opportunity to win some power by continuing to refuse the peas. It also tells her that sweets are a pleasure and peas are hard work.

Food as a reward or a punishment

Scientists have found that not only is it not particularly helpful to reward 'good' eating, it actually produces the *opposite* of the desired result. The implications of this cannot be overstated. Remember, if a reward is dependent on a particular food being consumed, this leads to an increased dislike of that food.[23] Rewarding your children for eating 'well' or for trying new foods is never a good idea.

The practice of offering rewards in the form of 'treat-foods' is not confined to the table. Many parents give their children an edible treat because of good behaviour. Superficially, this seems sensible - an ideal way to establish good habits like potty training (do a wee, have a jelly-bean…). But what is the message that the child will be picking up sub-consciously? It is this: "when I approve of you, I express this by giving you treat-foods".

In a similar way, sweets are often used as a means of offering comfort. For example, if a child is having an immunisation, it would be considered normal for a parent to give them a sweet or similar, in order to make the experience a little less upsetting. This comes from a place of care and kindness on the part of the parent but inadvertently merges edible treats and love.

In both of these scenarios, the child is picking up the following message subconsciously: "I have been given a sweetie. I'm okay, I feel loved". It is easy to imagine where this leaves him in adulthood. Let's take a brief detour into the world of adult comfort eating, also known as 'emotional eating'.

What is emotional eating?

Emotional eating has been defined as "eating in response to negative affect"[24]. In simple language, this means eating because you feel bad, not because you are hungry. The Priory Clinic in the UK did a survey which found that over 40% of adults admitted to eating due to loneliness, anxiety, sadness or stress[25]. That's nearly half of us. Of course, there are many factors involved in emotional or comfort eating and there are some interesting studies which examine what happens to our brain chemistry when we consume carbohydrates or fatty foods because we are stressed or unhappy. If we are taught as children to associate feeling good about ourselves with edible treats, this may well contribute to a habit of reaching for these foods when we feel a deficit of positive emotion.

Punishing with food

Giving children treats when they have been good leads to a sense of confusion between food and feelings, where treats equal love and approval. So what about punishing with food? This reinforces that same message from the other side of the coin. "You've behaved so badly in the park today that I'm not going to get you an ice cream" looks like clear and reasonable discipline. Why should you buy a child a treat when he has behaved appallingly? You wouldn't give him a treat following bad behaviour in any other context. Let's look again at the subtext. You are telling him that you do not approve of him and so he loses out on a sweet treat. Treat-foods, love and approval meet again.

Consider the following scenario, which will seem very outdated to most modern parents. The child is left at the table for hours on end until they 'clean' their plate. Here, a child is being punished for not eating a particular food leading them to associate that food strongly with negative emotions. It took me until my mid-twenties to even contemplate trying sweet corn after a particularly traumatic episode in school at the age of eight when I was made to sit by myself for what felt like hours, until I had eaten the last five kernels of sweet corn on the plate.

In practice

So having understood the theoretical side of how food and emotions can get mixed up together, how do you actually disentangle treats and a sense of being approved of in your child's mind?

First, look at the messages you are giving out about different foods. If you become a little more conscious about how you talk about food as a family, you can begin to eradicate beliefs about some foods being a pleasure and others a chore. Celebrate the cabbage as much as the dessert. Talk about the lovely soup you're serving with as much relish as the delicious ice cream you're having for pudding. As we'll see in the next chapter, how you talk about and react to food has a huge impact on your children.

Secondly, follow the next EAF principle:

EAF principle 3

• **Never use food to punish or reward**

This principle relates not just to behaviour, but also to using treat-foods as incentives to eat. For example, not giving a child dessert until he's eaten all his vegetables or bribing him to eat with promises of sweets.

Time for reflection

Take a moment to consider if food has ever been a symbol of love and approval in your life by thinking about these questions.

1) Was food ever used as a reward in your childhood?

2) Was food ever used as a punishment in your childhood?

3) Do you ever comfort-eat? If so, think about when, why and what you get from it.

4)   Do you ever use food to show your children that you approve or dis-
approve of their behaviour? If so, what other things could you use
instead?

One working mother I spoke to described how she used to buy her children sweets in her lunch break because it made her feel better about being away
from them. They loved having sweets on the way home from nursery and she
felt less guilty. It was only when she came to confront her ambivalent feelings
about working that she got an insight into what the sweets were really about.

What! No treats?

If, having read this, you have decided not to use food as a reward, you may
be left wondering if this means that edible treats are to be banished for good.
Absolutely not. The whole point about developing a good relationship with
food is that children can learn to think of eating as one of life's pleasures. From
a psychological perspective, there is nothing wrong with sweets, ice cream,
crisps and all the rest, in moderation and in the right context.

We have looked at the wrong context where they are confused with approval
and love. The alternative is to give occasional treats that are not conditional on
anything. Back to the park when the ice cream van arrives. Why not spontaneously buy your children an ice cream? This can be something to be enjoyed that
is in no way connected with their behaviour.

Many parents find that occasionally buying treats can lead to pleading. One
way around this is to have clear rules (again, this separates any potential links
between food and approval) so that children can predict when they'll get treats
and learn that there is no point asking for them at other times because the
answer will consistently be 'no'. One mother I know has a rule that her children
only eat sweets after lunch on a Saturday. They also have a packet of crisps each
from the vending machine after swimming once a week and a chocolate bar in
their lunch boxes every Thursday.

This works for her because she loves routine. Work out what's right for your
family - your snack policy has to fit in with your own beliefs about nutrition and

lifestyle. What is important, however, is to make sure that children only receive treats in a way that they cannot connect to being approved of or rewarded. Remember that the minute you begin saying that your child has to miss out on a treat because of her behaviour, you are making a link between eating unhealthy foods and approval. The minute you reward good behaviour with food, you are encouraging your child to fuse and confuse what they eat and how they feel about themselves.

Summary

- Dividing food into 'good' food and 'bad' food by using treats as an incentive to eat food perceived as undesirable may get short term results but actually makes picky eating worse

- You need to break the link between food and approval

- Comfort or emotional eating is about confusing eating and emotions. By giving your children a healthy relationship with food from a young age, you may lessen their chances of eating for comfort as an adult

- **EAF principle 3**
  Never use food to punish or reward

VII

Modelling

So far we have been looking at some key principles to follow whilst address-ing your child's picky eating

- Avoid either praising or criticising how or what your child is eating

- Stay calm and upbeat, keeping anger and anxiety away from the table

- Never use food to punish or reward

These principles underpin EAF, but you may be wondering what meal-times will actually look like if you decide to use this approach.

Let's look again at this EAF rule

1) **To avoid making food an issue before anyone's even sat down, never give any options - put everything on everyone's plate, in age appropriate portions**

Here's what you will achieve: by giving everyone a bit of everything, you have an opportunity to model, or demonstrate, positive eating behaviours.

Modelling is a term used by psychologists to describe a way of learning by watching what other people do. In the context of the family, what parents model has a much more powerful effect on children's behaviour than what parents say. This is where "do as I say, not as I do!" falls down.

Scientists have found that what children eat and patterns of behaviour around food are usually determined by parents. In fact, a child is much more likely to taste a food that he has first seen his parents eating[26]. This is logical really - we look to our parents to show us what is safe and what to avoid. Similarly, a child's acceptance of food is influenced by the example set by those around him, including siblings and anyone else who regularly eats with him[27], so the whole family needs to be on board before you embark upon EAF. In Chapter 14 where we discuss what has to be in place before you make any changes, we explore the best way to get significant others to sing from your song-sheet.

Time for reflection

What might you be modelling?

1) Think about which foods you really dislike - does your child share any of these preferences?

2) Think about why you dislike certain foods - have you ever heard your child mention the same reasons?

3) What messages about eating do you communicate to your child?

4) Does your child ever see you under- or over-eating?

5) Modelling is not just about dislikes - what foods do you enjoy eating? Does your child also consider them a treat?

EAF involves a little introspection on your part. Before you can expect your child to change, it's important to honestly assess whether you may be modelling any unhelpful or negative behaviours. If the answer to this question is "yes", or even "possibly", the next step is to consider how best to address this. If you feel that your issues are really deeply embedded you may choose to seek counselling. If you don't feel that this is such a big problem for you, it may be enough to have a frank conversation with your partner or a friend. This whole process is not easy and being ready to face your own demons is perhaps the hardest part.

I worked with a mum whose little boy, William (not his real name), would only eat ten foods - he was very threatened by texture and avoided anything slippery or wet. His mum had long suspected that she suffered from OCD (obsessive compulsive disorder) as she had a fear of germs and dirt. As we talked, it became apparent to her that the behaviour she was modelling conveyed the message that food could be dirty and dangerous and this was really affecting her son.

We worked together to look at ways of modelling different behaviour, showing William that mess and different textures are okay. She also accessed counselling so that she could work on her OCD with appropriate support. This is an extreme case, but it illustrates how your own behaviour influences your children.

Tasha Davis says "What you do is so much more powerful than what you say. Parents are the biggest influence on their children in their formative years, and modelling a positive attitude towards food is therefore essential. If you enjoy food and eat well, chances are, so will your children."

Not only is the behaviour you model important, but so is the behaviour of siblings or even grandparents and anyone else your child regularly eats meals with. Research shows that there is a clear connection between what foods a child will eat and what is eaten by the rest of the family[28].

Power and control

We have seen that giving everybody everything provides opportunities for positive modelling, but it will also help you beat picky eating for another reason. This concerns preventing your child from having opportunities to use food as an emotional lever. Requests for special treatment, for example, pasta with the mushrooms taken out, will become a thing of the past once your child knows that this is simply not house policy - no exceptions.

Many parents are quite happy to make small adjustments to their children's meals but this can be problematic. I can think of a mother who was so pleased that her picky son was eating salad at all, she was more than prepared to leave the tomatoes off his plate. However, apart from making you into what Americans call a 'short order chef', quickly preparing different dishes according to everyone's whim, this gives your child a kind of attention that rewards pickiness. It says "you are special and I will take extra time over your food" and gives your child power. Of course all your children are special and it's fine to take time preparing their food but what we're talking about here is not giving children the tools to engage in power play.

If everyone knows that they get everything on their plate regardless of personal preference, the potential for fuss diminishes. If your child reacts to the first sight of their tea with a disgusted: "yuk! - You know I hate broccoli" that can really affect the tone of the whole meal. It's rude - you have just spent time preparing this food (not to mention planning, shopping and paying for it) and this kind of negative comment will establish a combative dynamic that's hard to shift. If you reiterate, day in, day out, the fact that "everyone always gets everything - leave whatever you don't want", then requests for personalised meals will fade away.

A word on manners

This brings us to the third and final EAF rule, which overlaps with some of the ideas presented in Chapter 12 where we look at manners. It comes into play here because it gives you a practical way of eliminating fuss about food.

3) If you don't have anything positive to say about your dinner, don't say anything - it's not acceptable to criticise your food

If your child is old enough to grasp this, you might like to add the caveat to this rule that it's fine to say you don't like something if you've been asked. The aim here is to communicate to your child that she will not get attention for *complaining* about her food, as opposed to telling her that all opinions expressed have to be positive. If the whole family adheres to this rule, you will all be modelling a positive response to food which will rub off on your child. At the same time, you are ensuring that there is no pay-off in the form of attention for being rude or negative about what's being served up that day.

Teach your child how to politely and quietly leave food that he has chosen not to eat. He doesn't want his fish? No problem. He can leave it. The atmosphere remains calm and light and no-one is dwelling on who wants what. Compare this to the scene where your child refuses to eat his fish and you respond by trying to talk him into eating it. Everyone gets emotional and he gets a lot of attention, perhaps to the extent of dominating the meal.

At this point, you may feel uncomfortable because, when you have concerns about your child's eating, it can seem that getting him to eat something healthy is more important than the atmosphere at the table or whether he is gaining control via negative attention. These feelings are understandable but you need to think about your long-term goal. If your child can develop a good relationship with food, this will benefit him over the long-term more than a couple of extra mouthfuls of fish.

By reacting casually to his claims that he will not be eating his fish, you are also leaving him room to change his mind without losing face. It works like this - if you have engaged in a battle, he has to state his case: "I will not touch this fish!" Every argument from you makes him hold onto this position more forcefully as tempers fray. If it's not made into an issue, he can quietly try the fish when he thinks no one is looking, his pride intact.

Some families like to insist that everyone stays at the table until the meal is over. This can be really helpful. The boy who has refused the fish has to sit at the table for some time with his unfinished plate in front of him. As you're not going to give him attention for picky eating, the meal is proceeding calmly and everyone else is eating. This is when he starts to pick at the fish. Even if he spits it out, just the very act of trying it is progress. Remember, don't praise or reward or even comment on his trying it, just notice and feel pleased that he is one step closer to becoming a fish fan.

Summary

- What parents 'model' (or teach via how they behave) at the table has a powerful influence on children's behaviour, in fact a greater influence than the words they actually say

- **Teach your child EAF rule 3**
  If you don't have anything positive to say about your dinner, don't say anything - it's not acceptable to criticise your food

VIII

Keep on keeping on

This chapter is about climbing into your rhinoceros' hide and serving up food that your child doesn't like, again and again… and again. Giving a particular food on many different occasions is known as 'exposure'.

The importance of multiple exposures to new foods

Research shows that children show an increasing acceptance of a new food after repeatedly being exposed to it[29]. Interestingly, in another study[30] it was found that mothers were deciding that a child disliked a particular food after an average of less than three exposures. The number of exposures required for any real change in the child's negative response to a new food was up to ten. Another study places it even higher, at between 8 and 15 exposures[31]. The conclusion that can be drawn from this is that many parents may be giving up on a new food too quickly. Deciding that your child is picky and does not like something can become a self-fulfilling prophecy.

If you imagine that you may prepare a certain kind of food say, once every three or four weeks, this means that you would have to repeatedly offer it to your child for almost a year before you could say that she had a genuine aversion to it. However, rather than putting an excessive emphasis on what your child is eating by tracking the number of exposures she has had to any particular food type, it's preferable to just keep on relentlessly serving it up.

In fact, not only do you need to offer a child a disliked food many times before giving up on it, repeated exposure actually *increases* her liking of that food[32]. In the light of this research, giving everybody everything at every meal makes complete sense. You are maximising your child's exposure to disliked foods and increasing the chance that she will broaden the range of foods that she will eat.

Variety

A similar and related concept is variety. The most limiting factor when it comes to food preferences is unfamiliarity due to never having been offered a food[33]. In other words, the strongest influence on the likelihood of your child turning her nose up at avocado at school, is if she has never been offered avocado at home.

Giving your child a varied diet is vital to tackling picky eating. A large part of picky eating comes from a need for control and this need for control is sometimes underpinned by a sense of anxiety. So it follows that a child will feel safe when she is eating familiar foods and will feel out of her comfort zone when she is faced with new foods. Often, parents of picky eaters report that their child will only eat a particular category of foods, like foods with a certain texture or colour (nothing green... nothing wet...).

To borrow from the world of Cognitive Behavioural Therapy (CBT) which is a type of therapy that helps people to change how they think and behave, we can apply the principle that every time a person confronts the source of his anxiety, it weakens it and every time he avoids the source of his anxiety, that anxiety is reinforced. So every time you give your child beige foods for example (because those are within his comfort zone) you are confirming that green foods are threatening.

If you can manage to present your child with a wide variety of meals, even when you know she is unlikely to like them at first, you are making it much harder for problematic habits and food 'rules' like "I don't eat slippery foods" to become established. This can be really hard when you are worried about her nutritional needs - it may feel better to offer a plate of beige foods that you know will go down without a fuss, than go to time and trouble preparing varied meals that, in the short-term, will be rejected. However, when you use EAF, you are prioritising your child's long term food habits over what she consumes at that particular sitting.

Parents who have tried EAF have reported that this one of the hardest things to accept. You need to let go of the very natural focus on what your child eats at each meal and instead, take the long view. If you make your child a meal that doesn't cater to his particular preferences, he may only eat three mouthfuls. However, if these mouthfuls contain tastes and textures that are new to him, that's a better outcome than if he eats a plateful of a food that is within his comfort zone.

Modelling comes into play again in relation to the concepts of exposure and variety. With EAF, the habits of the whole family are important, not just those of the child. Think about the questions below and, if you are in the habit of offering a limited range of 'liked' foods, they may help you to process some of your very natural anxiety about breaking this pattern.

Time for reflection

1) Roughly how many different meals do you serve per month?

2) Do your child's food preferences limit the variety of food you serve?

3) How many times do you offer your child a new food before you decide he dislikes it?

4) How do you feel when you prepare something and your child rejects it?

5) What would be the hardest thing for you about making your child food you're almost certain she won't eat?

One mum wrote to me about the impact of this aspect of EAF on her five year old son. She said:

"We've decided to be more confident with cooking dishes we want to eat (rather than relying on the 'tried and tested' ones we know Jack likes). It's been really positive and he has eaten a variety of vegetables including runner beans, peas, carrots, chick peas, corn on the cob and lettuce, with a little suspicion at first but now without a fuss. I'm so happy about this little achievement and have realised that I wasn't really presenting the opportunities for him. As with most things, it's down to confidence! "

Summary

- Repeated exposure to disliked foods is a vital tool in the fight against picky eating

- Make sure you provide a varied diet for your family because being offering a wide variety of foods minimises pickiness

- You have to be tough when you use EAF - providing a varied diet and repeatedly exposing your child to disliked foods takes a lot of determination

IX

Appetite

Appetite is your friend. Appetite, rather than parental pressure should be the motivating factor behind a child's choice to eat. This harks back to the ideas about emotions and food, as well as food being used as a tool for manipulation or power play. If your child is eating because he is hungry rather than to please you, or even if he is leaving food because he does not feel hungry rather than to get a reaction from you, he is taking responsibility for his choices. Food and emotions are not tangled up together. As we saw in Chapter 2, appropriate hunger is okay and we don't need to worry so much about protecting our children from it.

According to the Gateshead Millennium Baby Study, genuinely poor appetites are rare in children[34]. It might seem that your child is never hungry, but perhaps the emotional issues around food have become so deep seated that he is not recognising his body's signals. Hopefully once you start to separate eating from the fight for control, power and attention, he will start to feel hungrier and his physical cues won't be obscured by his emotional needs.

On the other hand, a parent once told me that her little boy was so stubborn, he'd sooner starve than eat the same as the rest of the family. When eating is still about a battle of wills, I can imagine that this might be the case. However, once the child begins to understand that there's no pressure on him to eat and no loss of face from deciding to eat, he's probably going to be less inclined to see himself as embroiled in a battle which he has to win.

Self-regulation

Self-regulation (as it relates to appetite) means the process whereby we stop or start eating according to what our bodies tell us our needs are. Children naturally self-regulate, enabling them to control how much food they consume in accordance with their physical requirements.

An interesting study[35] showed that, when researchers covertly changed the energy content of pre-school children's first meal of the day, the children unconsciously made choices about what they consumed over the rest of the day so that their overall energy intake stayed the same. They automatically compensated for the changes the researchers made, ending up with the same energy intake at the end of a 30-hour period, regardless of what they'd been given to start off with. This demonstrates that children can and do self-regulate.

The natural process of self-regulation can be interfered with, however, if parents exert too much control over what their child eats. Cited in the same study, scientists found that (in a sample of mothers and daughters that they were studying) the greater the mothers' restriction of their daughter's diets, the less able the daughters were to self-regulate and the more likely they were to weigh more. This points to an interesting link between self-regulation and obesity. What can we take from this as parents? Giving your child responsibility for choosing whether she eats what she is given, not only removes the potential for power struggles and boundary testing at the dinner table, it also helps teach her how to self-regulate.

This is actually quite radical. Who knows best what your child needs to eat? Your child does. EAF is about trusting him to trust his body, enabling him to be in tune with his physiological cues. In this culture, we are programmed to make sure that our children eat enough of the right things. Really, our job is simply to provide those 'right things' at the right times and then hand over to the children. One day they'll have third-helpings, one day they'll skip a meal all together. It'll all be okay if this is internally not externally driven, i.e. their food choices are driven by their tummy not their mummy.

Clearly if you left a child entirely to her own devices, she might go for a chocolate bar on a bed of marshmallows for lunch, with a side order of ice cream. This is where you come in. EAF is not about the child dictating her own diet - you set the framework within which she makes her choices. It's fine to occasionally involve your child in your menu planning, but not if that results in a battle in which she is fighting for control over what you prepare. With EAF, you make tasty food at appropriate times and your child chooses how much and what to eat of what you have prepared.

This concept is what Registered Dietician Ellyn Satter[36], calls 'division of responsibility in feeding'. The division she is referring to is as follows: the parent's job is to provide healthy food at appropriate times and the child's job is to decide how much of that food to eat. For suggested further reading by Ellyn Satter, see the Resources section.

Appetising = appetite

At the risk of straying into the realms of nutritional advice which is not the purpose of this book, I feel that it is worth mentioning the importance of preparing appetising food for your child. I don't mean spending hours on elaborate dinosaur-themed pizzas, just cook food that tastes good. If you practice EAF, you will be serving your child the same as the rest of the family. Why give your child something you would not find appetising yourself?

One mum I talked to mentioned the impact of taking care over the presentation of family meals.

"I find that making food look good really pays off with my four. Not in a silly 'make it in a face shape' way, just genuinely taking a bit of care over the presentation, the way a chef does, to stimulate the appetite. I have found this makes a big difference with my kids and they often comment that it 'looks good' in an appreciative way" (Annabel, Lincoln, UK).

This goes back to the idea about questioning your role as a parent in relation to food. If you see your job as getting as much nutritious stuff down your child as possible, then offering an array of food items which are healthy but unconnected from a culinary perspective makes some kind of sense. However, if you want to focus on food as a social, enjoyable experience, make meals that make culinary sense and taste good. As one Dad I spoke to put it "I wouldn't want to eat a piece of yesterday's broccoli from the fridge and a random cherry tomato on a plate, so why would I offer it to my daughter?"(James, Brighton, UK). If you are offering tasty meals that are nicely presented, your child is much more likely to want to eat them.

An idea that's entrenched in our culture is that of 'children's food'. In reality, this often means bland, predictable food without much variety. There is no reason why children can't have the same food as adults, just in smaller portions. This used to be the case on the continent, although even in France now, there are often children's menus in restaurants featuring pasta, cheese and tomato pizza and other 'easy to eat' offerings. Children's menus are giving children the message that they should only like safe and familiar food.

Perhaps you are short of time or don't feel very confident about cooking. EAF is not about preparing complex meals or being tied to your kitchen. Just make sure that you offer a wide variety of meals. Prepare for your whole family the kind of food that you yourself want to eat. Whether that's a ready-meal or something you've made from scratch is irrelevant.

Summary

- Your child should be sitting down to meals hungry - hunger is a significant motivating factor when it comes to eating well

- Trust your child to self-regulate - children should listen to their bodies and eat or not eat according to their internal cues

- Make food appetising - why expect your child to eat something that you wouldn't consider tasty and visually appealing yourself?

X

Natural consequences

When you practice EAF, if your child has decided to leave some or all of her meal, you are faced with two possible scenarios. Perhaps your child doesn't need the food and so her choice to leave it is a healthy one. Perhaps she does need the food but is choosing to leave it in the (unconscious) hope that you will react in a particular way. Whichever scenario is true, **no reaction from you is required.** If it's the former, respect her ability to self-regulate. If it's the latter, teach her that she will have to take responsibility for the outcome of this decision by using 'natural consequences'. In either case, how you respond will be the same - stay relaxed and allow your child to make her own decision.

Earlier in the book, this EAF rule was introduced:

Leave whatever you don't want, but there are no snacks or alternatives later

Imagine for a moment that you are an intelligent four year old. You don't like the look of what's on your plate at dinner time and you know that if you kick up a fuss, or perhaps if you ask sweetly enough (trust me, you'll be well aware of what approach works best in your house) Mummy will make you some bread and jam instead.

What possible motivation could you have for eating your dinner? How much better to have some special attention, a sense of control *and* the yummy bread and jam. Let's imagine Mummy's not such a push-over. You know from past experience that you won't get an alternative, but if you hang on in there, you'll get a banana as a snack later so there's no negative consequences attached to leaving all of your meal. Again, why not leave the dinner and look forward to banana time?

Now imagine that your child knows that there are no snacks and no alternatives. If she decides to leave her meal, she will be hungry. This leaves the decision-making to her so you don't get emotionally embroiled in whether she decides to eat or not. There is no pay-off for her in terms of power play or attention, only the possible consequence of feeling hungry. A child is more likely to choose to eat if it's a simple choice between feeling hungry later and not feeling hungry, instead of an opportunity to test a boundary or get attention. This is an example of using what parenting experts call 'natural consequences'.

A natural consequence is something that happens naturally as a result of a choice your child makes. It is not a consequence that you, as the parent, impose. For example, if your child wants to walk to school without gloves, to allow the natural consequences to play out, you let him leave his gloves at home. His hands get cold because, guess what? It turns out your additional 30 years on the planet *have* taught you something and he learns that if you don't wear your gloves on chilly days, you get cold hands.

This is different from taking his gloves away so that he gets cold hands - that's simply a punishment and wouldn't be an appropriate form of discipline in any scenario. Natural consequences don't involve intervention by the parent. You say "okay, you make the choice" and he learns from the consequences of that choice. It is important to note that natural consequences are not sensible if the consequence places the child in danger or presents a health risk. Letting your small child experience the natural consequences of playing with a carving knife, for example, is not an appropriate or safe way to teach him not to touch sharp things.

Sue Wilson says "When using natural consequences to help your child learn about his behaviour, make sure that he is ready for this developmentally. Children usually start to connect behaviour with outcomes at about the age of three; however, they all mature at different rates. They also need to have sufficient grasp of language to be able to understand these ideas. You will have a sense of when your child is ready for this kind of approach."

If you stick to the rule that your child can choose to leave some or all of his lunch AND you allow the natural consequence to happen by not giving snacks or alternatives, your child will learn very simply that not eating what he's given may lead to feeling hungry. Consistency is vital - give in on this just once and you'll be faced with demands for snacks following a missed meal.

This is a theme that runs throughout EAF and if you stick to it, you won't go far wrong. Having made the decision that in your house, there is no food outside scheduled mealtimes and no one gets anything special or different, keep to it 100% always and forever. Very soon, your child will learn that leaving food can mean hunger later. Asking for snacks or alternatives isn't worth the bother because the answer is always 'no'.

If your child is too small to understand cause and effect, it's still important not to provide snacks or alternatives when she leaves or refuses food even though she won't yet gain any insight into the results of her choices. This is because her appetite alone will motivate her to eat at the next meal. In other words, if she rejects lunch, you want her to be hungry at dinner time so that she won't reject that too. Unfortunately, this may mean a miserable afternoon for you as hungry toddlers are not much fun. With EAF, you have to be patient and you have to be tough, but it'll be worth it.

Your schedule

Some parents may be feeling uncomfortable about not offering snacks, especially to younger children. Snacks are not off limits per se, only if your child is not eating well at main meals. Some health professionals suggest that it is preferable for toddlers to eat frequent, small meals. That's fine *if* they eat them. Draw up a schedule of meals and snacks that you feel is right for your family. If you want some advice on an age-appropriate schedule, your health visitor will be very happy to help with this. Imagine your schedule looks like this:

7:30	cereal
10:00	milk to drink

12:30	lunch
3:00	fruit snack
4:30	dinner
6:00	supper

If this works for you and your child is eating well and is not making a fuss at meal times, great. However, that seems unlikely given that you have made it to Chapter 10 of this book. If your child is always leaving his lunch, ask yourself whether you could drop the mid-morning milk. A 2007 study showed that excessive milk-drinking can affect appetite[37]. Just be careful that your child is getting enough dairy in her diet overall. Again, your health visitor can advise you on this. If your child is picky at tea time, drop the fruit snack for a week and see if things improve. It's all about trial and error and discovering what works best for your child.

Make sure that, when you experiment with dropping what was a scheduled snack, you don't couch it in terms of 'good food / bad food' as discussed in Chapter 6. For example, rather than telling your child that, on a given day, because he's been picky at breakfast, he won't be allowed an apple mid-morning, tell him that you're doing things differently these days and he'll be having fruit as pudding after lunch instead of as a snack.

You don't want to give the impression that you are punishing your child by denying him the good stuff. Think of it more as a policy change. You can always revert back if his pickiness subsides. As we've already seen, small children's dietary needs fluctuate over time and you need to be flexible. The key principle is that you don't want to be offering snacks that are allowing your child to avoid the natural consequence of feeling hungry when she has chosen to refuse food.

Snacking and Behaviour

A final issue concerning snacks has to do with snacking as a means of controlling behaviour. In our culture, food is often used as a way of keeping children entertained, keeping them quiet or simply keeping them 'out of trouble'. This is okay to a certain extent, if and only if it's not affecting their appetite at mealtimes. I'm not above a sly packet of raisins to keep my toddler from single-handedly ruining the Nativity Play, for example, but if this has become the norm, perhaps you have a problem.

A recent study found that mothers who used food to soothe their children had less confidence in their ability to parent than other mothers in the sample. They also rated their children as temperamentally more negative than average. This implies that, when a mother doubts her ability to manage a child, whether because of that child's challenging temperament, her ability to parent or both, food may be used as a means of controlling behaviour.[38]

If you believe that you sometimes use food as a means of managing your child's behaviour, spend some time working on alternative strategies. It's an easy habit to get into, but most parents will find that they have many other approaches that they know work with their child. If not, have a look at the 'Resources' section of this book under 'Parenting' for some suggested further reading. The following questions will help you think about whether you need to make any changes in this respect.

Time for reflection

1) Do your children know when they can expect snacks or do they get snacks as and when they want them?

2) Do you think that your child's appetite is ever 'spoiled' because he or she has been snacking before a meal?

3) Do you ever use snacks to make your life easier or to control behaviour? If so, how? Can you think of any alternative strategies that don't involve food?

One mum I spoke to said that she couldn't imagine how she was going to get her daughter into her pushchair without the use of snacks. Her little girl was very active and hated being strapped in anywhere, so this mum had, in her words "Pavlov's dogged" her, giving her a pack of raisins every time she had to go in the pushchair. Instead, she decided to put a sticker on a chart every time her daughter managed not to make a fuss and was very surprised at how easily this new strategy became the accepted routine. Sometimes the anticipation of how a child will react to a new rule is far worse than the reality. Children are flexible creatures, usually surprisingly ready to embrace a new way of doing things.

Summary

- Feeling hungry is the 'natural consequence' of choosing to leave food - if your child is developmentally able to make this connection, it can help him decide to eat what he's been given when this is what his body needs

- Devise your own food schedule and use trial and error to get it right for your child - you want her to have enough energy intake, whilst also coming to main meals hungry

- If snacks are being used as a means of behaviour management, consider alternative strategies

XI

The power of a label

The idea that labelling a child creates a self-fulfilling prophecy is not a new one. Somehow, there's something in the human psyche that makes us see what we expect to see in others and makes us live up to other's expectations. Clearly, this can be both positive and negative. The teacher who expects a lot from his or her pupils will convey that aspirational attitude and pupils will do well.

In one well-known experiment[39], scientists gave researchers two groups of rats with a maze to navigate. They told them that one group of rats was good at mazes and the other less so. In fact, they were all just normal rats with the same maze experience and ability. Lo and behold, the rats from the group labelled 'good at mazes' were perceived as more successful maze-navigators by the researchers. They saw what they expected to see.

Practitioners of a type of therapy called Transactional Analysis (TA) talk of childhood 'scripts'. These are the messages we take on about ourselves that derive from our childhoods, such as "I am the messy one". If you tell a child that he has a particular attribute, it can stick and will become part of his script. A person who has not been through the process of analysing his or her scripts and their origins may still be very much in their thrall. I still have to stop myself declaring that "I'm rubbish at maths" the minute I am faced with a numbers question. Actually, as an adult, I'm getting increasingly numerate as my confidence and experience grow. My first reaction, however, is still to bring out the old script.

Tasha Davis says "Everyone has their own role to play within the family, but a lot of the time it's the parents who are unconsciously directing the show. The more we label our children's behaviour, the more we may find that they live up to our negative expectations. By moving away from labels, we give our children more freedom and allow them to play a bigger part in writing their own scripts."

Here are some of the labels picky eaters are saddled with: 'faddy', 'fussy', 'bad-eaters', 'finicky', 'difficult' and of course 'picky'. The irony is not lost on me that I too am contributing to the labels business by using one myself… What happens when you label your child in this way? He takes on the script and behaves accordingly.

A sure-fire way of making sure your child won't try a new food is to tell her she won't like it. As a parent of a picky eater, it's easy to pre-empt a scene by telling friends and family at mealtimes, "Oh, don't give Zoe that, she won't like it". Zoe may never have tried it. Possibly Zoe won't like it, but if she's given some anyway, she may try it and begin going down the path of multiple exposures described previously.

This brings us to the final EAF principle

EAF principle 4

- **Never label your child 'picky', or speak critically about his or her eating**

If your child never hears you referring to him as picky, faddy and the rest, either directly in conversation with him or when you're talking to other people, he will be far less likely to take on the label and behave accordingly. Similarly, try to refrain from referring to other children as 'good eaters'. "Eat your spinach - Emily's eating her spinach, why can't you be a good eater like Emily?" This is not only a form of negative attention, it's also labelling by default. "If Emily's a good eater, then I must be a bad eater." Siblings in particular have a role to play. They should never be used as an example of a 'good eater'. They also shouldn't be allowed to comment on their brother's or sister's eating habits.

The blame game

Labelling can be used to locate all of the problems in the child. This can leave parents feeling that there is nothing they can do about their child's eating as the problem is innate. While there is evidence that children can have a genetic pre-disposition for sensitivity to certain foods and textures[40], that does not mean that there's nothing to be gained by looking at environmental factors.

Locating the problem solely in the child gives parents permission to avoid looking at how the family as a whole might be affecting the situation. It also implies that, if the problem does not lie within the family then neither does the solution. This harks back to that age-old debate - nature versus nurture. In the case of picky eating, as with most things, it's probably a little of both. Genes, we can't change, environment, we can.

Blaming the child is flawed, so where does this leave us? Blaming the parents? No. The chances are your child's problems are caused by a combination of personality and life experience. To blame yourself is counter-productive. It just leaves everyone feeling bad and guilt is not a particularly constructive emotion. Instead, take things from the present moment. Yes, there may be problems, yes, perhaps you as a parent have contributed to them but you are brave enough to tackle them head-on, otherwise you wouldn't be reading this.

Take time to look at the reflective exercises in this book and be honest in your responses, but please don't beat yourself up. EAF is about looking forwards not backwards. Accept what has gone before and feel good about your choice to confront your child's issues. You'll need to be feeling confident and resilient in order to carry out EAF consistently, so focus on gathering all your resolve for that, not wasting energy on self-blame.

The family food 'ethos'

Labelling gives rise to negative expectations that your child is likely to live up to. Similarly, how your family feels about mealtimes can become its own kind of self-fulfilling prophecy. This is connected with the ideas introduced earlier about keeping the mood at the table relaxed and upbeat, as well as the discussion in the next chapter which looks at how mealtimes can be positive social experiences.

Picture how you are feeling as you prepare a meal for a child who you expect will reject it. Imagine you are concerned about her health and worrying about your ability to manage the situation. It is not hard to envisage that, by the time you all sit down for the meal, you may be expecting a negative response. You are feeling angry / worried / frustrated / sad (delete as applicable). Perhaps other family members such as older siblings are feeling tense as they wait for the fireworks to commence. All of these feelings are very understandable.

Your challenge is not only to change your expectations of what your meal-times will be like, but also to try to shift the whole atmosphere around eating. If your family meals are predictably negative and stressful, you need to break that pattern. This goes back to the TA concept of family scripts. Your whole family will slip easily into their role at the table. Mum doing anxiety, Dad, anger. Big sister, bored indifference as she notices how her younger sibling is getting all the attention again. With all of this in place, it is an awful lot to expect the 'picky eater' to do anything other than act according to expectations.

Psychologists studying group dynamics have seen that within any group, certain roles are taken on by each member. Perhaps you can think back to your family as a child - was anyone 'the joker', 'the mediator', 'the devil's advocate'? In any kind of group, powerful forces are at work, driving individuals to unconsciously take on a particular function and families are no exception.

All of this demonstrates that it's really hard to break out of your family script and shake off the familiar roles that fit like a pair of favourite shoes. How can you change your family ethos and make meal-times positive experiences? First, look at your own emotional responses as described in Chapter 3. Secondly, put the fun back into food. Model a little excitement. For example, try some new recipes or involve the children in the cooking. Get everyone else onside so that any other adults or teenagers in the family are on-message and understand the importance of making mealtimes pleasant and relaxed.

Enforcing the rule about no-one making negative comments about food will help here. If the majority can focus on having a nice time, one child being fussy about what's on her plate will diminish into relative insignificance. Couple this with everything we've covered about not giving picky eating any attention and she'll soon be carried along by the mood of the majority.

This won't happen instantly and it will probably take a few meals to get the hang of it. Hold on to your brief - avoid the old script and aim for a relaxed and pleasant meal. If your child chooses not to eat her dinner, fine. That's her choice. Don't dwell on it, bring the attention back to someone who has something to say and keep the mood positive.

Perhaps mealtimes in your home are not group affairs and it might just be you and your child at the table. This makes things harder for you, as you are the only one responsible for lightening the atmosphere, keeping the conversation flowing and keeping the focus away from what's happening on your child's plate. If this is true for you, maybe you could call on supportive friends or family members to come and join in with your mealtimes occasionally. It's much easier to break a negative atmosphere with other people around to dilute it and visitors provide a welcome distraction from the "I'm not eating that!" show.

Of course, fun-packed mealtimes are not supposed to be the reality, day-in, day-out. EAF is not about making everything seem rosy all of the time, just a way of moving away from old roles at the table towards something different and new, where there is no room for lots of talk about who likes what, what looks 'yuk' and how many mouthfuls of cabbage anyone has eaten. It could be that you're having a lively debate or heated argument over dinner, or talking about something that happened at school that day. That's all fine, just keep the focus away from the food.

Time for reflection

1) What was your 'label' as a child, if you had one?

2) Can you think of any labels you may have imposed on your child or children, either positive or negative (excluding labels related to eating)?

3) Can you think of all the ways you may have labelled your child in the past, in relation to his or her eating habits?

If you conclude that you have been labelling your children in relation to eating, don't feel bad - almost every parent of a picky eater that I have spoken to has said that this is something they recognise. Once you make some small changes in the way you talk to and about your child in relation to their eating, the effect of any labels will begin to fade.

Summary

- Picky eating is caused by a combination of genetic and environmental factors - it is unhelpful to blame yourself, or to locate all of the problems in the child

- Foster a positive 'family food ethos' so that pleasant mealtimes become the norm and your child can break free of old roles where the focus of mealtimes was her eating

- **EAF principle 4**
  Never label your child 'picky', or speak critically about his or her eating

XII

The social side of food

There has been talk in the media about the benefits of eating as a family after a recent UK study found that even eating together as little as once or twice a week had an impact on how well children ate. Using a sample of more than two thousand children, researchers found that the children who always ate as a family consumed the recommended five daily portions of fruit and vegetables, the children who sometimes ate together consumed 4.6 portions and the ones who never ate as a family, 3.3.[41] These findings are striking, and confirm the belief that many experts have long held, that family meals are good for children.

Catherine Lee, in her guide to child development, writes "Meals are more than eating: they are social occasions, an important part of the civilisation in which the child is developing" [42]

In Chapter 7, we looked at 'modelling', the theory that how our children see us behaving has an enormous influence on how they behave. It makes sense that if children see us enjoying our food and using meals as an opportunity to chat and catch up with one another, they will follow suit. It is not enough just to be at the table as a family - you need to ensure that the mood is right. Very simply, the nicer the atmosphere, the more children eat[43]. In fact, scientists have found that there are many aspects of the way a family interacts during meal-times that influence how much family members eat, including how controlling parents are and how much conflict there is at the table[44].

This is not to imply that every family meal in your house needs to fit with a utopian vision of tinkling laughter and amusing anecdotes swapped as the children tuck into their broccoli. We're talking about a realistic, everyday nice atmosphere where the norm is calm and pleasant even if there's sometimes a bit of conflict or negativity. Donald Winicott[45] famously talked about the "good enough" mother - the idea that as long as, on the whole, a mother is in tune with her child and consistently providing good quality parenting with the odd minor blip, everything will turn out all right. The idea of good enough mealtimes is useful in this context. Don't aim for perfection because that's just another opportunity to make yourself feel guilty for not achieving the unachievable.

Equally, frequent family meals may be hard to manage in families with two working parents, or in single parent families where that parent has a full-time job. The point is not that you should feel guilty about not living on the set of 'The Waltons'. The point is that you need to look at your personal circumstances and within those, see if there's any room for manoeuvre. For example, eating your own dinner earlier with your child rather than eating after he's in bed could make an enormous difference.

Manners

A family meal is a social training ground - an opportunity for children to learn about how to behave in relation to other people. Manners are really just culturally determined rules that ensure that people are considerate of one another in the way that they behave. They are about controlling behaviour in order to adhere to socially accepted norms. What you expect from your children in terms of manners is very much up to you, but here are a few thoughts.

First, if your child has issues with eating and does not enjoy mealtimes, focusing on her manners is not going to help that situation. Especially with younger children, I would suggest that it's best to forget all about manners. Let her eat with her fingers, chew with her mouth open or play with her food. Make your primary aim to ensure that the atmosphere at the table is as relaxed and positive as possible and that the focus is taken away from food and eating. If you are constantly reminding your child that she needs to remember her manners, it can be very hard to achieve these aims.

You can begin to work on manners once the picky eating starts to improve and you have reliably happy mealtimes together. Decide with your partner if you have one, which rules matter to you and which don't, so that you are consistent in your approach and don't fight battles that don't need fighting. For example, some parents can't tolerate their children putting their elbows on the table but this doesn't bother me. I insist that my children hold their knife as well as their fork but I have friends who are happy for everyone just to use a fork. It's all fine, just decide what works for you and your family.

Catherine Lee[46] suggests teaching table manners away from the table using play. You could have a teddy bears' picnic putting your child in charge of the teddy bears' manners. You could have a pretend meal with 'food' made of things from the garden and demonstrate your best etiquette. You know your child and can no doubt think of imaginative ways of teaching manners through play that will engage her.

Social skills

Social skills are akin to manners but are more about learning behaviours that are transferable to everyday life. These include turn-taking, listening and developing empathy. At the table, a child learns by watching the adults, observing how they behave around food as well as their attitudes to one another[47]. If you compare a child that always eats his main meal alone or in front of the television, to one who has several meals a week eating communally, the first child is missing out on a huge number of opportunities to learn social skills.

Teaching social skills happens naturally and unconsciously on the whole, mostly through effective modelling. However, if you find that your meals are not consistently relaxed and pleasant, you can try a few more systematic approaches to help your child take part in positive social interactions. For example, you could go round the table getting everyone, including you, to talk about something they've done that day. This involves listening and turn-taking. One mother I spoke to found that this didn't work for her as her children replied with the familiar refrain "nothing!" But when she asked them to tell her the worst bit of their days, they were much more forthcoming…

If you notice that your children are great at talking but not so great at listening, you could use mealtimes as an opportunity to teach them new skills in this area. Make sure you model good listening skills yourself as this is the best way to teach a child. You could consider some clear directions that will help improve good communication. For example, if one person at the table shares something about their day, you could encourage your child to ask a question about it before sharing her own news. Children are naturally focused on what they have to say and practising listening to others before jumping in to talk about themselves is a really valuable lesson.

Distraction

Finally, keeping the focus on conversation enables you to move everyone's attention away from what and how your child is eating. In Chapter 3, we talked about the pay-offs that children get from both positive and negative attention. When you give a child any kind of attention for their eating, you are potentially making picky eating worse. Parents have amazing powers of distraction, perfected in the early days when it's still possible to distract a toddler from the fact that you have just taken back your car keys or whatever his latest unsuitable treasure may have been. Use these skills at the table. If your child is focusing on his meal in a negative way, engage him in conversation, move things on and keep the mood light.

Summary

- When you are tackling your child's picky eating, forget about manners for the time being - this will make it easier to foster a relaxed atmosphere at the table

- Work on improving manners away from the table through play

- Eating together as a family can really help with picky eating

- Use mealtimes as an opportunity to develop your child's social skills

XIII

Start as you mean to go on

Maybe you are expecting a baby and have an older child who has issues with eating. Maybe you are the parent of a small baby and are reading this book to learn about how to give your child a good relationship with food from the word 'go'. Either way, this chapter is for you.

If you are tackling picky eating with an older sibling and do not want the picky behaviour to rub off on your little one, remember the rule about not allowing negative things to be said about the food. You are separating behaviour from eating here - it's appropriate to be strict about this whilst still allowing your child to choose not to eat what he does not like. Even if your baby cannot talk, he will soon understand what his big brother means when he looks at his meal and shouts "gross!"

On the other hand, don't despair if your older child is refusing food in front of your baby as you can counteract this with the positive behaviour around food that you and other adults model. Also, by ignoring picky eating you will show the younger sibling that this is not an effective way of getting attention.

Baby-led weaning

Baby-led weaning is an approach to giving children solids that is gaining in popularity amongst parents. It has recently had some exposure in the media after a UK study showed that children who feed themselves as babies are less likely to be obese than those who are spoon-fed, because they learn to self-regulate[48]. There are several ways in which baby-led weaning resonates with EAF.

In brief, baby-led weaning involves giving your baby a selection of solid foods at mealtimes and allowing her to choose for herself what she eats, rather than spoon-feeding her. No purees, just a selection of foods that she can manage, often cut into 'chip' shapes so she can grasp them easily. This approach begins at the very start of the weaning process so it isn't appropriate for parents who have chosen to wean earlier than the recommended age of six months, because a baby will not be developmentally ready to feed himself before this age.

Gill Rapley[49] introduced the term 'baby-led weaning' in 2008, to describe this method of offering solids. For details of her books, see the Resources section. It is outside the remit of this book to give an in-depth account of this technique and you need to read up about it, go to classes or get advice from a health professional before trying it. This is because it's important to ensure that the food you offer your baby is age-and-stage-appropriate.

Nutritional Therapist Kathryn Barker (who runs Baby-Bites weaning classes) says "Baby-led weaning embraces the natural eating behaviours of a child. Young children may well eat a lot one day and nothing the next, or choose not to eat something for weeks then suddenly it's their favourite food. Baby-led weaning accepts this natural behaviour and doesn't question it. It also works with the 'safety features' Mother Nature created babies with, such as the gag reflex which gradually moves further back as babies get older and more used to manipulating food around the mouth. For me it's illogical to teach a baby to swallow food (purees) before they have learnt to chew food. Baby-led weaning puts the transition on to solid food in line with nature, in a very organic process, when the baby is developmentally ready"

One aspect of baby-led weaning that fits in with EAF is that you can give your baby the same food that the rest of the family eats. This will require a little bit of thought and planning to ensure that it's suitable for him, for example, not adding salt to your cooking and not giving him anything that is too hard or tough for him to manage.

Baby-led weaning sits well with many of the principles of EAF - your baby will feel part of a social occasion if he is sitting at the table feeding himself the same food at the same time as everyone else. He will get the variety and the multiple exposures that he needs if he eats the same menu as everyone else.

He will learn to self-regulate and get into a pattern of choosing what to eat and what to leave as his body dictates.

Before Solids

Going back to the very beginning, how you feed your baby also makes a difference to her relationship with food in later life. As discussed earlier, when parents are controlling in their approach to what their child eats, this can result in his relying on external rather than internal cues to make decisions about how much food to ingest, which in turn has been linked to obesity and picky eating[50]. Interestingly, children who are underweight and whose parents closely control and monitor what their children consume, end up more underweight than other children who are also underweight but whose parents are not controlling at the table[51].

Research into the reasons why parents come to develop a controlling or restrictive approach to feeding their children has shown that mothers who breast-feed are less likely to exert control over their children's food intake by the time their child is one year old. Moreover, mothers who breast-feed longer are less controlling than those who stop breast-feeding early[52]. Researchers speculate that the decision to stop breast-feeding early may be driven by anxiety about a child's weight gain, which makes sense in the light of the link between parental anxiety and a controlling approach to food.

Breast-feeding can also facilitate the acceptance of a wider variety of foods. In one study, breast-fed and formula-fed babies were given pureed vegetables to eat. Although there was no difference in how the babies reacted to the vegetables at first, after ten exposures, the breast-fed babies consumed significantly more vegetables than their formula fed counterparts[53]. The theory is that formula provides babies with just one flavour experience, whereas the taste of breast milk is always changing according to what the mother is eating. This ties in with findings about the importance of multiple exposures to food and the importance of a varied diet[54].

As discussed in Chapter 4, breast-feeding is an emotive topic. It is absolutely inappropriate to judge a mother on her decision to breast-feed or formula-feed. Often, that decision is not made lightly and is the result of potentially traumatic problems with the establishment of successful breast-feeding. I know from experience how hard that can be, as having breast-fed my first two children until about 12 months of age, my third baby always struggled with feeding. Despite getting lots of support from my health visitor, friends and family, I decided to switch to formula. She's was fine and I was fine, but I certainly had to work through my initial feelings of failure and guilt at not giving my youngest the same experience that I had given her sisters.

Pregnancy

Going even further back in time, a mother's diet in pregnancy also plays its part in shaping her unborn child's relationship with food. A 2007 study found that when pregnant mothers were given repeated drinks of carrot juice in their third trimester, their babies showed less negative facial expressions when fed carrot flavoured cereal than the babies in the study whose mothers were not given carrot juice.

"A growing body of evidence suggests that the food choices a mother makes during her pregnancy may set the stage for an infant's later acceptance of solid foods...... this early experience can provide a 'flavor bridge' that can begin to familiarize the infant with flavors of the maternal diet."[55]

I have often wondered if it is more than coincidence that my eldest child is crazy about pickled herrings and Chinese egg fried rice when this is what I craved constantly whilst I was carrying her. Possibly not the best example of a varied diet during pregnancy!

Summary

- Baby-led weaning is an approach to weaning where babies feed themselves - it fits with many of the ideas contained within EAF

- What you eat when you're pregnant can influence your unborn child's preferences

- Breast-fed babies get a wider taste experience than formula-fed babies, which can facilitate the acceptance of new foods

XIV

Ready for change?

The ideas behind EAF are simple, but that doesn't mean that applying them is easy. In fact, the longer that particular patterns of behaving have been in place, the more entrenched they become and the harder they are to shift. However, small children are very malleable and the good news is that, if you have sufficient resources and determination, your child's habits can be dramatically modified.

In the introduction there was a warning against starting to use EAF without having first read the whole book. Now that you have gained a thorough understanding of this approach, you need to make a decision about the best time to begin. Factor in how resilient you and your partner (if you have one) are feeling. Think about timing - if you are planning a family holiday or have other changes in environment on the horizon, could that help or hinder? You may want to wait until you're back in your normal routine or you may feel that a change of scene will make all these new ideas easier to implement. The questions later in this chapter will help you decide.

You can't do this by yourself

Before you begin using EAF, it is vital that you get everyone important in your child's life on side. First, your nuclear family. Has your partner read the book? Is he or she as committed as you are? Make sure you've ironed out any disagreements before you begin. If your child has older brothers or sisters, perhaps you could explain the situation to them.

Many people have problems persuading relatives to alter their patterns of behaviour. One mum I spoke to had made significant changes to mealtimes in her own home but as soon as they went to Grandma's, her son was being offered a chocolate bar in return for eating his main course. Understandably, she was furious as she watched all her hard work being undermined. Clashes like this will give rise to tension between family members which is the last thing you need, so try to have the discussion (away from your child) before you begin.

Don't underestimate how supportive your child's school or nursery can be. Make an appointment to speak to his teacher and explain what you are going to be doing at home. Many children eat several meals a week at school and it will be confusing to them if they are getting conflicting messages about their behaviour from their teachers and their parents.

Jackie Vallance, assistant head at a UK primary school, with many years' experience, says "A good home/school relationship is always important but when things are not going quite as expected, it becomes even more so. Children have a whole range of issues to deal with when in school - friendships, routines, rules and relationships to name but a few. We, as teachers, want to make school life a happy and positive experience. Building a good, open relationship with parents is vital.

We can offer support, guidance and a sympathetic ear to parents, carers and families. We can reinforce strategies used at home and provide opportunities for discussion within the class in a discreet and anonymous way. This helps many children to identify with similar or parallel issues. Discussing mealtimes, food and the social setting into which they fit, often helps other pupils who may have anxieties or misunderstandings themselves.

Teachers would welcome an insight into the problems your child is encountering. Working together on any difficulty means the problem is shared. Teachers are happy to listen and would be interested to receive guidance from other professionals. If you are having a particularly tricky time let us know. If things are going well, and there is a strategy that is working well, again, let us know. We all want happy, confident and sociable children, whether in home or school - let's work together to achieve this."

Time for reflection

1) On a scale of 1 - 10, where 1 is 'very low' and 10 is 'on top of the world' how positive, energised and resilient are you feeling at the moment?

2) Take some time to make a list of all the people in your child's life who you need to get on side. How do you feel each person will support you?

3) Is anything coming up over the next few weeks and months that will make starting EAF especially challenging for you or your child, such as a house move, changes to your childcare arrangements or your job?

4) If you are in a relationship, what does your partner think about EAF? Are you both equally committed?

5) What potential pitfalls can you see in the road ahead?

6) What do you want to achieve with EAF? Write your hopes for your child's relationship with food in an envelope and open it in 12 months' time so you can see if you've achieved your goals. More technically-minded readers can schedule an email to be sent to them in a year's time.

7) On a scale of 1-10, how committed are you to making this work, where 1 is 'very hesitant' and 10 is 'absolutely, 100%'?

Having chosen a start date, explain to your child that things are going to be changing. In an age-appropriate and low-key way, let her know what the new rules are. You don't need to get into much detail, just tell her when she can expect meals and snacks, that she can leave whatever she wants but there are no unscheduled meals or alternatives and that everyone will be eating the same thing.

Rate of Change

Some parents ask whether they should introduce change gradually or all at once. In terms of the EAF rules and principles, you should try to make these changes all at once, explaining to your child that things need to be different in order for everyone to enjoy happy mealtimes.

In terms of what you put on your child's plate, start giving everyone the same immediately but use your judgement when it comes to meal planning. If the foods your child will accept are very limited indeed, plan a week's meals including all his favourites as well as a few more challenging items thrown in. Gradually expand your repertoire so that he is gently being introduced to new tastes.

If your child's food issues are more minor and her picky behaviour is not always consistent (for example, one day she makes a fuss about bits in her yoghurt, next week she eats her yoghurt but complains about the mashed potatoes) go the whole way and offer all the family the meals that you want them to be eating, regardless of how well you think this will be received. You know your child best - use your judgement about when to bring in more challenging and unfamiliar menus. Whatever you choose to serve, always give the whole family the same meal and put everything on everyone's plate.

Be consistent

As with other aspects of parenting, if you can be consistent, you have won most of the battle. The importance of never deviating from the EAF practices that you have learned cannot be overstated. If you give your child a snack because he's hungry having refused his dinner, he will always have a spark of hope that you will waver again. Any chink in your armour gives him an opportunity to engage in power play and has the potential to confuse him. You must be clear and consistent, 100% of the time. Obviously this can be really difficult, which is why you'll need to pick the right time to start EAF and you'll need as much support in place as possible.

Magic wands only exist in fairy tales

This is not a quick fix, magic bullet, magic wand or any other form of instant answer to your child's eating problems. EAF involves potentially profound changes to your family's food habits as well as a fair bit of reflection and honest soul-searching on your part. It takes time, it takes energy and there will be many lows before the highs.

Expect things to get worse before they get better. Whenever a child is met with new boundaries, her first reaction is to challenge them. She wants to test them, to see how far they go and whether they are real and permanent. For example, you may be refusing snacks or alternatives for the first time. Your child will feel outraged as something she used to take for granted has been withdrawn. After two or three weeks of consistent EAF, she will learn that these changes are for real and you will hopefully start to see some improvements.

First steps

You have already made the biggest change of all, just by acknowledging that there is a problem, buying this book and reading it to the end. It takes real courage to admit that things aren't right, especially if part of that admission involves examining the role you may have unwittingly played in the situation. Having faced the problem and looked for a solution, you have come a very long way. Good luck! You are embarking on a journey that may result in significant changes in your child's eating habits. The gift of a positive relationship with food is one of the most valuable things a parent can give a child and it will last a lifetime.

Feedback

Other parents would love to hear how you've got on, so please visit the EAF blog to share your experiences.

You can find it at: www.ea-feeding.com

Appendix A
A case study

Susie and Matt (all names have been changed) are a couple in their 30s, both working part time. They have two small children. Angus is five and in his first year at primary school and Edie is a lively two year old. Susie approached me because she had started to notice that Angus was becoming picky about his food and mealtimes were often unpleasant, with Angus immediately reacting negatively to the food Susie offered him.

To begin with I asked Susie about her food history. She was a little taken aback and said she loved food and had no issues with eating. However, after Susie and I went through some questions (reproduced in Chapter 4) it became clear that, although she loves food now, it had been a source of distress for her as a child.

Susie described how her mother was relatively passive and had health problems whilst her father was angry and controlling. Susie shared her worst memory about food: she did not like onions and so one day picked out all of the onions from her dinner and ate the rest; her father made her stay at the table for hours until she had eaten the onions.

Similarly, Susie acknowledged that her mother used food in a dysfunctional way, only cooking meals that she herself liked (a limited selection of foods) whilst ignoring Susie's personal preferences and nutritional needs. Susie sensed the injustice in this. Until she was an adult preparing her own meals, there were many foods that she'd never been exposed to, such as certain kinds of green vegetable. When Susie was an adolescent, the dinner table was an unhappy place - family meals were dominated by arguments as she and her father had extremely different political views which gave rise to constant clashes.

Susie's authoritarian father's need to control what and how Susie ate, her mother's blindness to Susie's personal preferences and the unpleasant nature of mealtimes have affected her as an adult. Susie has made sure that her own children do not experience any of these things. She described how she cooks a wide variety of different foods for her children. She respects their likes and dislikes and does not make them eat what's on their plates. She sometimes offers alternatives if they reject what they've been given. Her parenting style is calm and kind and her children are well balanced and happy and yet Angus was making mealtimes extremely difficult for everyone.

When I asked Susie to tell me more about Angus' behaviour, she described how he would angrily say "yuk - I'm not eating that" when he first saw his meal. We looked at separating eating behaviour from manners and I explained that being strict about the rule concerning not being rude about food is very differ-ent from being authoritarian in terms of what a child consumes. Susie felt that she had perhaps confused her desire to avoid mimicking her father's controlling behaviour with maintaining appropriate discipline at the table. In other words, she let Angus respond to his food like that because she didn't want to be like her father.

I explored with Susie what Angus might be gaining in terms of attention through his negative remarks and picky eating. At first, she felt sure that this was not about attention - she is aware of how positive and negative attention work and did not feel that these ideas were relevant here. After a pause, how-ever, Susie had an insight into what might be going on. She realised that the evening meal was the first time that she and her husband sat down together all evening and they used the evening meal as an opportunity to catch up.

Susie acknowledged that Angus was potentially not getting the attention he needed as she and Matt had so much to say to each other. She decided to try focusing on Angus more during the meal in such a way that there was still room for adult conversation but Angus felt included. We speculated that Angus used his behaviour around food as a way to tell his parents "hey! I'm here too you know!"

The hardest aspect of EAF for Susie to embrace was the idea that it would be okay to let Angus go hungry if he chose to leave all or part of his meal.

Although she is a great supporter of teaching children through natural consequences in other areas, when it came to food, she found it difficult to let him
experience hunger, perhaps because it felt punitive due to what she had been
through as a child.

Susie and Matt began using EAF techniques with Angus and almost immediately they found that things were getting better. The first improvement was to
do with the atmosphere at the table. Once Susie stopped feeling anxious about
Angus' food consumption, she began to relax as did everyone else. Angus is a
bright little boy and was old enough to take on board the new rule about not
being rude about his dinner. Being a generally confident parent, Susie was well
able to use her normal discipline techniques to implement this.

Angus reacted positively to the increased attention at the table that he
gained from being involved in the conversation. Susie and Matt managed to
find other times to talk about work. Eventually, the pattern at the table moved
from Matt and Susie chatting, Angus hijacking it and Susie getting anxious and
angry, to everyone enjoying one another's company without the exaggerated
focus on what Angus was putting in his mouth. Angus still chooses to leave
things and he's still relatively cautious about what he will and won't eat, but
mealtimes are happy occasions now and things continue to improve.

My thanks to Matt and Susie for letting me include their story.

Appendix B
Special cases

Sometimes, parents are facing challenges with their children's eating that go beyond what might be described as straightforward 'picky eating'. If this is true for you, you will need more specialist information and support than can be found in this book. Aspects of EAF may be useful to you, but make sure you access appropriate professional input that is tailored to your child's needs. The following are examples of special cases where feeding can be particularly difficult. This is not detailed information or advice.

Autistic Spectrum Disorder (ASD)

Children with ASD frequently have eating problems. This can be for several reasons. It is wrong to imply that all children with ASD experience the same issues around food as each child will have their own unique set of challenges. However, many children with this diagnosis are hypersensitive, which means that they react far more intensely to sensory stimulation that their neuro-typical counterparts. This hypersensitivity could be in response to smell, texture, temperature, taste or visual stimuli. Clearly all of these senses are engaged in the process of eating, so mealtimes can prove overwhelming for these children.

Another feature of ASD is difficulty in social situations. It is easy to imagine how (in a school setting for example) a communal meal could pose several problems. The environment may be noisy and potentially very stressful to an autistic child as well as the social expectations that come with eating with others.

Polly Walker, a primary teacher who has specialised in working with children with special needs, says "It is very important to try and identify what lies behind feeding difficulties presented by a child with ASD. Once you have a deeper understanding of the reasons why your child is refusing a certain food or eating a restricted diet you will be better equipped to address things. Autistic children are generally very resistant to change and often it will take a great deal of patience and very many small steps before progress can be made. A child may need to be introduced to a new flavour/texture/colour/temperature of food in a series of stages and then may need support to apply this to different situations and settings. You will need to be consistent with your approach as children with ASD find familiar routines helpful and reassuring.

It is also worth bearing in mind that some children with additional needs may require support to actually learn how to chew and swallow different types of food. Health Professionals or Portage Workers are ideally placed to provide advice in this situation."

EAF will not be appropriate for an autistic child with eating problems - clearly more specialist help would be required. However, EAF could be used to help you stay calm and relaxed at mealtimes and understand how your child's behaviours may be affecting you and the rest of the family. With a child with ASD, it's vital to respect her need for rules around food. This does not mean you cannot try to improve the situation with professional guidance, but don't treat an autistic child's 'pickiness' as power play - it is more useful to see it as part of being autistic.

Diabetes

If your child has diabetes, EAF techniques will also not be appropriate for you. It's not okay to let a child with diabetes miss a meal and parents of diabetic children will no doubt be keenly aware of exactly what their child needs to consume and when. It can be really frightening for the parents of a diabetic child who refuses food. Remember that your anxiety will feed into the situation, so try to stay calm and upbeat. You will of course have to have specialist help if you are in this situation.

Most diabetic children have type one diabetes, but in Europe and America, not only are cases of type one diabetes on the rise, but we are also beginning to see more cases of type two diabetes, in line with increasing levels of obesity.

Diet plays a vital role in the management of diabetes so picky eating can be really challenging and stressful for parents.

Looked after children

If you are a UK foster carer looking after a child who has experienced abuse, especially neglect, you will need to approach things in a way that is more specifically tailored to the individual child. This will be in the context of the general plan for his or her care, ideally with expert professional input via CAMHS. As a foster carer, I cared for a toddler who had experienced neglect and as a result, needed very careful care around eating. For example, she could not cope with a whole plate of food in front of her because she found it over-whelming, so I used to put it near her, mouthful by mouthful, gradually giving her more and more at a time.

A child who has experienced neglect or a very chaotic lifestyle (where meals may well not have been predictable or regular) is likely to have complex issues around food. The aspects of EAF that deal with creating a relaxed and positive atmosphere at the table and examining your own feelings and attitudes could certainly be useful in this instance, alongside support from your health visitor, supervising social worker and the child's social worker. Please note: I would never recommend letting a looked-after child go hungry as it may echo previous abusive situations that they had experienced.

Obese children

If your child is clinically obese, you will need help from a qualified nutritionist or dietician. According to government figures, 30% of children aged between 2 and 15 are obese in the UK today[56]. In the US, the figure is very similar[57]. Alongside professional input, use EAF to help you try to understand your own food legacy as well as the role that family scripts may be playing in your child's eating. If your child has trouble with self-regulating and does not recognise when he is full, you may have to limit what he eats by only offering him portions that accord with his nutritional needs as advised by a professional.

Underweight children

If a health professional has diagnosed your child as being underweight, again, you will probably need the help of a qualified nutritionist or dietician. You can use several aspects of EAF - keeping mealtimes relaxed and positive, gaining an understanding of the role positive and negative attention can play and thinking about your own food history. It would not be appropriate, however, to let an underweight child miss a meal unless so advised by a professional.

In Summary

This book is written for the parents and carers of children without a medical diagnosis. If your child has medical or mental health issues that have been identified by a professional, aspects of EAF may be useful to you but you will need additional expert input.

Resources

Parenting

Carolyn Webster-Stratton - The Incredible Years: A Trouble-Shooting Guide for Parents of Children Aged 2 - 8 Years

Sarah Ockwell-Smith - ToddlerCalm: A guide for calmer toddlers and happier parents

Division of responsibility in feeding

Ellyn Satter - Feeding with Love and Good Sense - The first two years

Ellyn Satter - Secrets of Feeding a Healthy Family: How to Eat, How to Raise a Healthy Family, How to Cook

Website: www.ellynsatterinstitute.org

Children's nutrition (recommended by nutritional therapist Kathryn Barker)

Patrick Holford & Deborah Colson - Optimum Nutrition for Your Child: How to boost your child's health, behaviour and IQ

Patrick Holford & Fiona McDonald Joyce - Smart Food for Smart Kids: Easy recipes to boost your child's health and IQ

Baby-led weaning

Gill Rapley & Tracey Murkett - Baby-led Weaning: Helping Your Baby to Love Good Food (*for UK readers*)

Gill Rapley & Tracey Murkett - Baby-Led Weaning: The Essential Guide to Introducing Solid Foods and Helping Your Baby to Grow Up a Happy and Confident Eater (*for US readers*)

Gill Rapley & Tracey Murkett - The Baby-led Weaning Cookbook: Over 130 delicious recipes for the whole family to enjoy

Website: http://www.rapleyweaning.com/

Eating disorders

Glenn Waller, Victoria Mountford, Rachel Lawson & Emma Gray - Beating Your Eating Disorder: A Cognitive-Behavioral Self-Help Guide for Adult Sufferers and their Carers

Websites: www.b-eat.co.uk
www.nhs.uk/conditions/eating-disorders

Crib Sheet

The EAF principles

1. Avoid either praising or criticising how or what your child is eating

2. Stay calm and upbeat, keeping anger and anxiety away from the table

3. Never use food to punish or reward

4. Never label your child 'picky', or speak critically about his or her eating

The EAF Rules

1) To avoid making food an issue before anyone's even sat down, never give any options - put everything on everyone's plate, in age appropriate portions

2) It is fine for your child to leave anything he or she doesn't want to eat, but there will be no alternatives and no unscheduled snacks later

3) Teach your child
If you don't have anything positive to say about your dinner, don't say anything - it's not acceptable to criticise your food

References

[1] Reported in UK press, Daily Mail. Study of 1005 British mothers with children under 5, carried out by GrowingUpMilkInfo.com (dated 13/01/13)

[2] C. Wright, K. Parkinson, D. Shipton & R. Drewett (2007) **How Do Toddler Eating Problems Relate to Their Eating Behavior, Food Preferences, and Growth?** Pediatrics Vol. 120, No. 4, pp.1069-1075

[3] Daniel Mattila in radio interview with Jesse Leon, 'We're all Ears', New York, USA , March 2012. http://radionews.2012.journalism.cuny.edu/2012/03/19/cognitive-therapist-daniel-mattila-on-picky-eating/

[4] The International **HabEat** project: http://www.habeat.eu/

[5] http://www.rcpsych.ac.uk/pdf/76_5.pdf   (accessed 02/11/13)

[6] H. Duerr (May 22nd, 2013) **Experts Discuss Changes, Updates in DSM-5** Psychiatric Times http://www.psychiatrictimes.com/apa2013/experts-discuss-changes-updates-dsm-5 (accessed 02/11/13)

[7] Y. Martins, (2002) **Try it, you'll like it! Early dietary experiences and food acceptance patterns**. The Journal of Pediatric Nutrition and Development, Vol. 98, No.12-16, pp. 18-20

[8] S. Johnson, (2002). **Children's food acceptance patterns: The interface of ontogeny and nutrition needs**. Nutrition Reviews, Vol. 60, pp. S91-S94

[9] M. Cathey, N. Gaylord (2004) **Picky Eating: A Toddler's Approach to Mealtime** Pediatric Nursing, Vol. 30, No.2, pp. 101-109

[10] B. Carruth, J. Skinner, K. Houck, J.Moran III, F. Coletta & D. Ott (1998) **The Phenomenon of "Picky Eater": A Behavioral Marker in Eating Patterns of Toddlers**. Journal of the American College of Nutritionists, Vol.17, No. 2, pp. 180-186

[11] C. Wright, K. Parkinson, D. Shipton & R. Drewett (2007) **How Do Toddler Eating Problems Relate to Their Eating Behavior, Food Preferences, and Growth?** Pediatrics, Vol. 120, No. 4, pp. 1069-1075

[12] **Nutrition for Health & Health Care** (2007) ed. E. Noss Whitney, Thompson Learning Inc., p. 298

[13] C. Wright, K. Parkinson & R. Drewitt, (2006) **How Does Maternal and Child Feeding Behavior Relate to Weight Gain and Failure to Thrive? Data From a Prospective Birth Cohort**, Pediatrics Vol. 117, No. 4 April 1, 2006

[14] P. Costanzo, E. Woody (1985) **Domain-specific parenting styles and their impact on the child's development of particular deviance: The example of obesity proneness.** Journal of the Society of Clinical Psychology, Vol. 3, pp. 425-445

[15] S. Severe (1997) **How to Behave So Your Children Will Too,** Library of Congress, USA

[16] http://www.supernanny.co.uk/Advice/-/Food-and-Nutrition/-/0-to-4-years/Coping-with-a-Fussy-Eater.aspx (accessed 28/10/13)

[17] E. Lee, **Health, morality, and infant feeding: British mothers' experiences** (2007) **of formula milk use in the early weeks.** Sociology of Health & Illness, Vol. 29, pp. 1075-1090

[18] Figure from NICE, UK, cited online at http://www.b-eat.co.uk/about-beat/media-centre/facts-and-figures/ (accessed 28/10/13)

[19] Based on the statistic that 30 million people in the US suffer from an eating disorder at some point in their lives. http://www.nationaleatingdisorders.org/get-facts-eating-disorders (accessed 28/10/13)

[20] J. Lipps Birch, D. Wolfe Marlin & J. Rotter (1984) **Eating as the "Means" activity in a contingency: Effects on Young Children's Food Preference**, Child Development, Vol. 55, No. 2, pp. 431-439

[21] J. Newman & A. Taylor (1992) **Effect of a means-end contingency on young children's food preferences** Journal of Experimental Child Psychology, Vol. 53, No. 2, pp. 200-216

[22] **Daily Mail, (UK)** http://www.dailymail.co.uk/health/article-2253798/Sixty-cent-toddlers-hooked-sweets-according-Vitabiotics-Wellkid-Baby-Drops-research.html (dated 27/12/12)

[23] J. Lipps Birch, D. Wolfe Marlin & J. Rotter (1984**) Eating as the "Means" activity in a contingency: Effects on Young Children's Food Preference**, Child Development, Vol. 55, No. 2, pp. 431-439 (op.cit.)

[24] S. Nguyen-Rodriguez, C. Chou, J. Unger and D. Spruijt-Metz (2008) **BMI as a moderator of perceived stress and emotional eating in adolescents**, Eating Behaviors, Vol. 9, Issue 2, pp. 238-246

[25] www.comforteating.com

[26] B. Carruth & J. Skinner (2000) **Revisiting the Picky Eater Phenomenon: Neophobic Behaviors of Young Children**, Journal of the American College of Nutritionists, Vol. 19, No. 6, pp. 771-780

[27] B. Carruth, J. Skinner, K. Houck, J. Moran III, F. Coletta & D. Ott (1998) **The Phenomenon of "Picky Eater": A Behavioral Marker in Eating Patterns**

of Toddlers. Journal of the American College of Nutritionists, Vol.17, No. 2, pp. 180-186 (op.cit.)

[28] J. Skinner, B. Carruth, J. Moran III, K. Houck, J. Schmidhammer, A. Reed, F. Coletta, R. Cotter and D. Ott (1998) **Toddlers' Food Preferences: Concordance with Family Members' Preferences**, Journal of Nutrition Education, Vol. 30, Issue 1, pp. 17-22

[29] S. Sullivan, L. Birch (1994) **Infant Dietary Experience and Acceptance of Solid Foods,** Pediatrics, Vol.98, No.2, pp. 271-277

[30] B. Carruth, J. Skinner, K. Houck, J.Moran III, F. Coletta & D. Ott (1998) **The Phenomenon of "Picky Eater": A Behavioral Marker in Eating Patterns of Toddlers**. Journal of the American College of Nutritionists, Vol.17, No. 2, pp. 180-186 (op. cit.)

[31] B. Carruth, P. Ziegler, A. Gordon & S. Barr (2004) **Prevalence of picky eaters among infants and toddlers and their caregivers' decisions about offering a new food**, Vol. 104, No. 1 Supplement to The Journal of the American Dietetic Associations, pp. 57-S64

[32] S.Sullivan, L.Birch (1994**) Infant Dietary Experience and Acceptance of Solid Foods**, Pediatrics, Vol.98, No.2, pp. 271-277

[33] J. Skinner, B. Carruth, J. Moran III, K. Houck, J. Schmidhammer, A. Reed, F. Coletta, R. Cotter and D. Ott (1998) **Toddlers' Food Preferences: Concordance with Family Members' Preferences**, Journal of Nutrition Education, Vol. 30, Issue 1, pp. 17-22 (op. cit.)

[34] Wright, K. Parkinson, D. Shipton & R. Drewett (2007) **How Do Toddler Eating Problems Relate to Their Eating Behavior, Food Preferences, and Growth?** Pediatrics, Vol. 120, No. 4, pp. 1069-1075 (op. cit.)

[35] J. Savage, J. Orlet Fisher and L. Birch (2007) **Parental Influence on Eating Behavior, Conception to Adolescence**. Journal of Law and Medical Ethics, Vol. 35 (1), pp. 22-34

[36] www.ellynsatterinstitute.org

[37] C. Wright, K. Parkinson, D. Shipton & R. Drewett (2007) **How Do Toddler Eating Problems Relate to Their Eating Behavior, Food Preferences, and Growth?** Pediatrics Vol. 120, No. 4, pp.1069-1075 (op. cit.)

[38] C. Stifter, S. Anzman-Frasca , L. Birch, K. Voegtline (2011) **Parent use of food to soothe infant/toddler distress and child weight status. An exploratory study** Appetite, Vol. 57(3), pp. 693-9

[39] R. Rosenthal & K. Fode (1963). **The effect of experimenter bias on the performance of the albino rat**. Behavioral Science, Vol. 8, pp. 183-189

[40] M. Faith, Moonseong Heo, K. Keller A.Pietrobelli. **Child food neophobiais heritable, associated with less compliant eating, and moderates familial resemblance for BMI**. International Journal of Obesity, accepted but unpublished article. DOI: 10.1002/oby.20369

[41] M. Christian, C. Evans, N.Hancock, C. Nykjaer, J. Cade (2012) **Family meals can help children reach their 5 A Day: a cross-sectional survey of children's dietary intake from London primary schools**. Journal of Epidimiology and Community Health, Vol. 67, No.4

[42] Catherine Lee (1990) **The Growth & Development of Children**, 4th Ed. , Longman, London & NY

[43] D.Burnier, L.Dubois, M. Girard (2011) **Arguments at Mealtime and Child Energy Intake**, Journal of Nutrition Education and Behavior, Vol. 43, No. 6, pp. 473-481

[44] B. Carruth, J. Skinner, K. Houck, J.Moran III, F. Coletta & D. Ott (1998) **The Phenomenon of "Picky Eater": A Behavioral Marker in Eating Patterns**

of Toddlers. Journal of the American College of Nutritionists, Vol.17, No. 2, pp. 180-186 (op. cit.)

[45] D. Winnicott (1964) **The Child, the Family and the Outside World,** Pelican, England

[46] Catherine Lee (1990) **The Growth & Development of Children**, 4th Ed. , Longman, London & NY (op. cit.)

[47] Ibid.

[48] www.dailymail.co.uk/health/article-2097486/Giving-babies-finger-food-stop-growing-fat.html (dated 07/02/12)

[49] Gill Rapley & Tracey Murkett (2008) **Baby-led Weaning: Helping Your Baby to Love Good Food** Vermillion, London, UK

[50] J. Carper, J. Orlet Fisher& L. Birch **Young girls' emerging dietary restraint and disinhibition are related to parental control in child feeding** Appetite, Vol. 35, No. 2, pp. 121-129

[51] M. Faith, R. Berkowitz, V. Stallings, J. Kerns, M. Storey & A. Stunkard (2004) **Parental Feeding Attitudes and Styles and Child Body Mass Index: Prospective Analysis of a Gene-Environment Interaction**, Pediatrics Vol. 114 No.4, pp. e429 - e436

[52] J. Blisset & C. Farrow (2007) **Predictors of maternal control of feeding at 1 and 2 years of age,** International Journal of Obesity, Vol. 31, pp. 1520-1526

[53] J. Savage, J. Orlet Fisher and L. Birch (2007) **Parental Influence on Eating Behavior, Conception to Adolescence**. Journal of Law and Medical Ethics, Vol. 35 (1), pp. 22-34 (op. cit.)

[54] S. Sullivan, L. Birch (1994) **Infant Dietary Experience and Acceptance of Solid Foods,** Pediatrics, Vol.98, No.2, pp. 271-277 (op. cit.)

[55] J. Savage, J. Orlet Fisher and L. Birch (2007) **Parental Influence on Eating Behavior, Conception to Adolescence**. Journal of Law and Medical Ethics, Vol. 35 (1), pp. 22-34 (op. cit.)

[56] www.gov.uk/government/policies/reducing-obesity-and-improving-diet (accessed 15/06/13)

[57] www.frac.org/initiatives/hunger-and-obesity/obesity-in-the-us/ (accessed 28/10/13)

Printed in Great Britain
by Amazon